Ninja Air Fryer Cookbook for Beginners 2021

1000-Days Easy & Delicious Recipes for Beginners and Advanced Users. Easier, Healthier, and Crispier Food for Your Family & Friends

Julia Adamo

TABLE OF CONTENTS

Introduction

Ever since Ninja Foodi has stepped into the world of kitchen appliances, the company has introduced people to a range of multipurpose cooking appliances. Ninja Air fryer is one such example that has made waves of popularity due to its easy to use control panel and super-efficient Air frying mechanism. The device looks simple enough, yet it needs detailed guidance to tackle all sorts of troubleshooting situations. Every electric kitchen device should be used with care and smartness to enjoy a luscious meal every time. Here is why this cookbook offers a little guidance about the Ninja Air Fryer. Along with a set of scrumptious recipes, which are all created by experts using the Ninja Air Fryer.

Ninja Air fryer

If you look at any model of the Ninja Air fryer, you would instantly recognize it due to its distinct shape, size, and exterior. Unlike multipurpose cookers, this Air fryer has a simple mechanism to cook. The entire unit consists of a base which contains all the heating system along with a space to insert the basket carrying food. It is this easy to use a system that makes the Air fryer ultra-smart and convenient for all of its users. All a person needs to do is to add food to the basket and insert the basket back in its place. Select the appropriate temperature and timing to cook the meal, and then the machine does the rest for you. Ninja Air fryer is available in four different models currently:

1. AF100
2. AF101
3. AF101C
4. AF101CCO

The AF100 does not come with a multilayer rack to accommodate food in two layers inside the cooking basket; the rest of the models are provided this rack, which makes cooking even more convenient. People assume that with every model, the size of the Fryer basket changes, which is hardly true because all of the models provide equal-sized base units and fryer baskets.

Breakfast Recipes

Pumpkin Muffins

Prep Time: 15 minutes.
Cook Time: 13 minutes.
Serves: 8
Ingredients:

- ½ cup pumpkin puree
- 1 cup gluten-free oats
- ¼ cup honey
- 1 medium egg beaten
- ½ teaspoon coconut butter
- ½ tablespoons cocoa nib
- ½ tablespoons vanilla essence
- Cooking spray
- ½ teaspoon nutmeg

Preparation:

1. At 375 degrees F, preheat your Air Fryer on Air fry mode.
2. Add oats, honey, eggs, pumpkin puree, coconut butter, cocoa nibs, vanilla essence, and nutmeg to a bowl and mix well until smooth.
3. Divide the batter into the muffin tray, greased with cooking spray.
4. Place the muffin tray in the Air Fryer Basket.
5. Return the Air Fryer Basket to the Air Fryer and cook for 13 minutes.
6. Initiate cooking by pressing the START/PAUSE BUTTON.
7. Allow the muffins to cool, then serve.

Serving Suggestion: Serve the muffins with hot coffee.

Variation Tip: Add raisins and nuts to the batter before baking.

Nutritional Information Per Serving:
Calories 209 | Fat 7.5g |Sodium 321mg | Carbs 34.1g | Fiber 4g | Sugar 3.8g | Protein 4.3g

Air Fried Sausage

Prep Time: 10 minutes.
Cook Time: 13 minutes.
Serves: 4

Ingredients:

- 4 sausage links, raw and uncooked

Preparation:

1. At 390 degrees F, preheat your Air Fryer on Air fry mode.
2. Place the sausages in the Air Fryer Basket.
3. Return the Air Fryer Basket to the Air Fryer and cook for 13 minutes.
4. Initiate cooking by pressing the START/PAUSE BUTTON.
5. Serve warm and fresh.

Serving Suggestion: Serve the sausages with toasted bread and eggs.

Variation Tip: Add black pepper and salt for seasoning.

Nutritional Information Per Serving:
Calories 267 | Fat 12g |Sodium 165mg | Carbs 39g | Fiber 1.4g | Sugar 22g | Protein 3.3g

Cinnamon Toasts

Prep Time: 15 minutes.
Cook Time: 8 minutes.
Serves: 4

Ingredients:

- 4 pieces of bread
- 2 tablespoons butter
- 2 eggs, beaten
- 1 pinch salt
- 1 pinch cinnamon ground
- 1 pinch nutmeg ground
- 1 pinch ground clove
- 1 teaspoon icing sugar

Preparation:

1. At 390 degrees F, preheat your Air Fryer on Air fry mode.
2. Add two eggs to a mixing bowl and stir cinnamon, nutmeg, ground cloves, and salt, then whisk well.
3. Spread butter on both sides of the bread slices and cut them into thick strips.
4. Dip the breadsticks in the egg mixture and place them in the Air Fryer Basket.
5. Return the Air Fryer Basket to the Air Fryer and cook for 8 minutes.
6. Initiate cooking by pressing the START/PAUSE BUTTON.
7. Flip the French toast sticks when cooked halfway through.
8. Serve.

Serving Suggestion: Serve the toasted with chocolate syrup or Nutella spread.

Variation Tip: Use crushed cornflakes for breading to have extra crispiness.

Nutritional Information Per Serving:
Calories 199 | Fat 11.1g |Sodium 297mg | Carbs 14.9g | Fiber 1g | Sugar 2.5g | Protein 9.9g

Morning Egg Rolls

Prep Time: 15 minutes.
Cook Time: 13 minutes.
Serves: 6

Ingredients:

- 2 eggs
- 2 tablespoons milk
- Salt, to taste
- Black pepper, to taste
- 1/2 cup shredded cheddar cheese
- 2 sausage patties
- 6 egg roll wrappers
- 1 tablespoon olive oil
- 1 cup of water

Preparation:

1. At 375 degrees F, preheat your Air Fryer on Air fry mode.
2. Grease a small skillet with some olive oil and place it over medium heat.
3. Add sausage patties and cook them until brown.
4. Chop the cooked patties into small pieces. Beat eggs with salt, black pepper, and milk in a mixing bowl.
5. Grease the same skillet with 1 teaspoon olive oil and pour the egg mixture into it.
6. Stir cook to make scrambled eggs.
7. Add sausage, mix well and remove the skillet from the heat.
8. Spread an egg roll wrapper on the working surface in a diamond shape position.
9. Add a tablespoon of cheese at the bottom third of the roll wrapper.
10. Top the cheese with an egg mixture and wet the edges of the wrapper with water.
11. Fold the two corners of the wrapper and roll it, then seal the edges.
12. Repeat the same steps and place the rolls in the Air Fryer Basket.
13. Return the Air Fryer Basket to the Air Fryer and cook for 13 minutes.
14. Initiate cooking by pressing the START/PAUSE BUTTON.
15. Flip the rolls after 8 minutes and continue cooking for another 5 minutes.
16. Serve warm and fresh.

Serving Suggestion: Serve the rolls with your favorite hot sauce or cheese dip.

Variation Tip: Add crispy bacon to the filling.

Nutritional Information Per Serving:
Calories 282 | Fat 15g |Sodium 526mg | Carbs 20g | Fiber 0.6g | Sugar 3.3g | Protein 16g

Spinach Egg Muffins

Prep Time: 10 minutes.
Cook Time: 13 minutes.
Serves: 4

Ingredients:

- 4 tablespoons milk
- 4 tablespoons frozen spinach, thawed
- 4 large egg
- 8 teaspoons grated cheese
- Salt, to taste
- Black pepper, to taste
- Cooking Spray

Preparation:

1. At 390 degrees F, preheat your Air Fryer on Air fry mode.
2. Grease four small-sized ramekin with cooking spray.
3. Add egg, cheese, spinach, and milk to a bowl and beat well.
4. Divide the mixture into the four small ramekins and top them with salt and black pepper.
5. Place the ramekins in the Air Fryer Basket.
6. Return the Air Fryer Basket to the Air Fryer and cook for 13 minutes.
7. Initiate cooking by pressing the START/PAUSE BUTTON.
8. Serve warm.

Serving Suggestion: Serve the muffins with toasted bread slices and crispy bacon.

Variation Tip: Add sliced bell peppers to the muffins.

Nutritional Information Per Serving:
Calories 237 | Fat 19g |Sodium 518mg | Carbs 7g | Fiber 1.5g | Sugar 3.4g | Protein 12g

Pepper Egg Cups

Prep Time: 15 minutes.

Cook Time: 18 minutes.

Serves: 4

Ingredients:

- 2 bell pepper, halved, seeds removed
- 4 eggs
- 1 teaspoon olive oil
- 1 pinch salt and black pepper
- 1 pinch sriracha flakes

Preparation:

1. At 390 degrees F, preheat your Air Fryer on Air fry mode.
2. Slice the bell peppers in half, lengthwise, and remove their seeds and the inner portion to get a cup-like shape.
3. Rub olive oil on the edges of the bell peppers.
4. Place them in the Air Fryer Basket with their cut side up and crack 1 egg in each half of bell pepper.
5. Drizzle salt, black pepper, and sriracha flakes on top of the eggs.
6. Return the Air Fryer Basket to the Air Fryer and cook for 18 minutes.
7. Initiate cooking by pressing the START/PAUSE BUTTON.
8. Serve warm and fresh.

Serving Suggestion: Serve the cups with toasted bread slices and crispy bacon.

Variation Tip: Broil the cups with mozzarella cheese on top.

Nutritional Information Per Serving:

Calories 183 | Fat 15g | Sodium 402mg | Carbs 2.5g | Fiber 0.4g | Sugar 1.1g | Protein 10g

Morning Patties

Prep Time: 15 minutes.
Cook Time: 13 minutes.
Serves: 4

Ingredients:

- 1 lb minced pork
- 1 lb minced turkey
- 2 teaspoons dry rubbed sage
- 2 teaspoons fennel seeds
- 2 teaspoons garlic powder
- 1 teaspoon paprika
- 1 teaspoon of sea salt
- 1 teaspoon dried thyme

Preparation:

1. At 390 degrees F, preheat your Air Fryer on Air fry mode.
2. In a mixing bowl, add turkey and pork, then mix them together.
3. Mix sage, fennel, paprika, salt, thyme, and garlic powder in a small bowl.
4. Drizzle this mixture over the meat mixture and mix well.
5. Take 2 tablespoons of this mixture at a time and roll it into thick patties.
6. Place the patties in the Air Fryer Basket, then spray them all with cooking oil.
7. Return the Air Fryer Basket to the Air Fryer and cook for 10 minutes.
8. Initiate cooking by pressing the START/PAUSE BUTTON.
9. Flip the patties in the basket once cooked halfway through.
10. Serve warm and fresh.

Serving Suggestion: Serve the patties with toasted bread slices.

Variation Tip: Ground chicken or beef can also be used instead of ground pork and turkey.

Nutritional Information Per Serving:
Calories 305 | Fat 25g | Sodium 532mg | Carbs 2.3g | Fiber 0.4g | Sugar 2g | Protein 18.3g

Breakfast Bacon

Prep Time: 10 minutes.
Cook Time: 14 minutes.
Serves: 4

Ingredients:

- ½ lb of bacon slices

Preparation:

1. At 390 degrees F, preheat your Air Fryer on Air fry mode.
2. Spread the bacon slices in the Air Fryer Basket evenly in a single layer.
3. Return the Air Fryer Basket to the Air Fryer and cook for 14 minutes.
4. Initiate cooking by pressing the START/PAUSE BUTTON.
5. Flip the crispy bacon once cooked halfway through, then resume cooking.
6. Serve.

Serving Suggestion: Serve the bacon with eggs and bread slices

Variation Tip: Add salt and black pepper for seasoning.

Nutritional Information Per Serving:
Calories 273 | Fat 22g |Sodium 517mg | Carbs 3.3g | Fiber 0.2g | Sugar 1.4g | Protein 16.1g

Crispy Hash Browns

Prep Time: 10 minutes.
Cook Time: 13 minutes.
Serves: 4

Ingredients:

- 3 russet potatoes
- ¼ cup chopped green peppers
- ¼ cup chopped red peppers
- ¼ cup chopped onions
- 2 garlic cloves chopped
- 1 teaspoon paprika
- Salt and black pepper, to taste
- 2 teaspoons olive oil

Preparation:

1. At 390 degrees F, preheat your Air Fryer on Air fry mode.
2. Peel and grate all the potatoes with the help of a cheese grater.
3. Add potato shreds to a bowl filled with cold water and leave it soaked for 25 minutes.
4. Drain the water and place the potato shreds on a plate lined with a paper towel.
5. Transfer the shreds to a dry bowl and add olive oil, paprika, garlic, and black pepper.
6. Make four flat patties out of the potato mixture and place them in the Air Fryer Basket.
7. Return the Air Fryer Basket to the Air Fryer and cook for 13 minutes.
8. Initiate cooking by pressing the START/PAUSE BUTTON.
9. Flip the potato hash browns once cooked halfway through, then resume cooking.
10. Once done, serve warm.

Serving Suggestion: Serve the hash with toasted bread slices and crispy bacon.

Variation Tip: Add herbed cream on top of the hash browns.

Nutritional Information Per Serving:
Calories 190 | Fat 18g |Sodium 150mg | Carbs 0.6g | Fiber 0.4g | Sugar 0.4g | Protein 7.2g

Biscuit Balls

Prep Time: 10 minutes.
Cook Time: 18 minutes.
Serves: 6

Ingredients:

- 1 tablespoon butter
- 2 eggs, beaten
- ¼ teaspoons pepper
- 1 can (10.2 oz) Pillsbury Buttermilk biscuits
- 2 ounces cheddar cheese, diced into ten cubes
- Cooking spray
- Egg Wash
- 1 egg
- 1 tablespoon water

Preparation:

1. At 375 degrees F, preheat your Air Fryer on Air fry mode.
2. Place a suitable non-stick skillet over medium-high heat and cook the bacon until crispy, then place it on a plate lined with a paper towel.
3. Melt butter in the same skillet over medium heat. Beat eggs with pepper in a bowl and pour them into the skillet.
4. Stir cook for 5 minutes, then remove it from the heat.
5. Add bacon and mix well.
6. Divide the dough into 5 biscuits and slice each into 2 layers.
7. Press each biscuit into 4 inches round.
8. Add a tablespoon of the egg mixture at the center of each round and top it with a piece of cheese.
9. Carefully fold the biscuit dough around the filling and pinch the edges to seal.
10. Whisk egg with water in a small bowl and brush the egg wash over the biscuits.
11. Place the biscuit bombs in the Air Fryer Basket and spray them with cooking oil.
12. Return the Air Fryer Basket to the Air Fryer and cook for 14 minutes.
13. Initiate cooking by pressing the START/PAUSE BUTTON.
14. Flip the egg bombs when cooked halfway through, then resume cooking.
15. Serve warm

Serving Suggestion: Serve the eggs balls with crispy bacon.

Variation Tip: Add dried herbs to the egg filling.

Nutritional Information Per Serving:
Calories 102 | Fat 7.6g |Sodium 545mg | Carbs 1.5g | Fiber 0.4g | Sugar 0.7g | Protein 7.1g

Snacks and Appetizers Recipes

Onion Rings

Prep Time: 10 minutes.
Cook Time: 22 minutes.
Serves: 4

Ingredients:

- ¾ cup all-purpose flour
- 1 teaspoon salt
- 1 large onion, cut into rings
- ½ cup cornstarch
- 2 teaspoons baking powder
- 1 cup low-fat milk
- 1 egg
- 1 cup bread crumbs
- 1/6 teaspoons paprika
- Cooking spray
- 1/6 teaspoons garlic powder

Preparation:

1. At 375 degrees F, preheat your Air Fryer on Air fry mode.
2. Mix flour with baking powder, cornstarch, and salt in a small bowl.
3. First, coat the onion rings with flour mixture; set them aside.
4. Beat milk with egg, then add the remaining flour mixture into the egg.
5. Mix them well together to make a thick batter.
6. Now dip the floured onion rings into the prepared batter and coat them well.
7. Place the rings on a wire rack for 10 minutes.
8. Spread bread crumbs in a shallow bowl.
9. Coat the onion rings with breadcrumbs and shake off the excess.
10. Set the coated onion rings in the Air Fryer Basket.
11. Spray all the rings with the cooking spray.
12. Return the Air Fryer Basket to the Air Fryer and cook for 22 minutes.
13. Initiate cooking by pressing the START/PAUSE BUTTON.
14. Flip once cooked halfway through, then resume cooking
15. Season the air fried onion rings with garlic powder and paprika.
16. Serve.

Serving Suggestion: Serve with tomato sauce or cream cheese dip.

Variation Tip: Use crushed cornflakes for breading to have extra crispiness.

Nutritional Information Per Serving:
Calories 229 | Fat 1.9 |Sodium 567mg | Carbs 1.9g | Fiber 0.4g | Sugar 0.6g | Protein 11.8g

Cauliflower Gnocchi

Prep Time: 15 minutes.
Cook Time: 17 minutes.
Serves: 5

Ingredients:

- 1 bag frozen cauliflower gnocchi
- 1 ½ tablespoon olive oil
- 1 teaspoon garlic powder
- 3 tablespoons parmesan, grated
- 1/2 teaspoons dried basil
- Salt to taste
- Fresh chopped parsley for topping

Preparation:

1. At 400 degrees F, preheat your Air Fryer on Air fry mode.
2. Toss gnocchi with olive oil, garlic powder, 1 tbsp parmesan, salt, and basil in a bowl.
3. Place the gnocchi in the Air Fryer Basket.
4. Return the Air Fryer Basket to the Air Fryer and cook for 10 minutes.
5. Initiate cooking by pressing the START/PAUSE BUTTON.
6. Toss the gnocchi once cooked halfway through, then resume cooking.
7. Drizzle the remaining parmesan on top of the gnocchi and cook again for 7 minutes.
8. Serve warm.

Serving Suggestion: Serve with tomato or sweet chili sauce.

Variation Tip: Use crushed cornflakes for breading to have extra crispiness.

Nutritional Information Per Serving:
Calories 134 | Fat 5.9g |Sodium 343mg | Carbs 9.5g | Fiber 0.5g | Sugar 1.1g | Protein 10.4g

Peppered Asparagus

Prep Time: 10 minutes.

Cook Time: 16 minutes.

Serves: 6

Ingredients:

- 1 bunch of asparagus, trimmed
- Avocado or Olive Oil
- Himalayan salt, to taste
- Black pepper, to taste

Preparation:

1. At 390 degrees F, preheat your Air Fryer on Air fry mode.
2. Place the asparagus in the Air Fryer Basket.
3. Toss the asparagus with salt, black pepper, and oil.
4. Return the Air Fryer Basket to the Air Fryer and cook for 16 minutes.
5. Initiate cooking by pressing the START/PAUSE BUTTON.
6. Serve warm.

Serving Suggestion: Serve with mayonnaise or cream cheese dip.

Variation Tip: Use panko crumbs for breading to have extra crispiness.

Nutritional Information Per Serving:

Calories 163 | Fat 11.5g |Sodium 918mg | Carbs 8.3g | Fiber 4.2g | Sugar 0.2g | Protein 7.4g

Crispy Tortilla Chips

Prep Time: 15 minutes.
Cook Time: 13 minutes.
Serves: 8

Ingredients:

- 4 (6-inch) corn tortillas
- 1 tablespoon Avocado Oil
- Sea salt to taste
- Cooking spray

Preparation:

1. At 390 degrees F, preheat your Air Fryer on Air fry mode.
2. Spread the corn tortillas on the working surface.
3. Slice them into bite-sized triangles.
4. Toss them with salt and cooking oil.
5. Place the triangles in the Air Fryer Basket in a single layer.
6. Return the Air Fryer Basket to the Air Fryer and cook for 13 minutes.
7. Initiate cooking by pressing the START/PAUSE BUTTON.
8. Toss the chips once cooked halfway through, then resume cooking.
9. Serve and enjoy.

Serving Suggestion: Serve with guacamole, mayonnaise, or cream cheese dip.

Variation Tip: Drizzle parmesan cheese on top before Air Frying.

Nutritional Information Per Serving:
Calories 103 | Fat 8.4g | Sodium 117mg | Carbs 3.5g | Fiber 0.9g | Sugar 1.5g | Protein 5.1g

Fried Halloumi Cheese

Prep Time: 10 minutes.
Cook Time: 12 minutes.
Serves: 6

Ingredients:

- 1 block of halloumi cheese, sliced
- 2 teaspoons olive oil

Preparation:

1. At 360 degrees F, preheat your Air Fryer on Air fry mode.
2. Place the halloumi cheese slices in the Air Fryer Basket.
3. Drizzle olive oil over the cheese slices.
4. Return the Air Fryer Basket to the Air Fryer and cook for 12 minutes.
5. Flip the cheese slices once cooked halfway through.
6. Serve.

Serving Suggestion: Serve with fresh yogurt dip or cucumber salad.

Variation Tip: Add black pepper and salt for seasoning.

Nutritional Information Per Serving:
Calories 186 | Fat 3g |Sodium 223mg | Carbs 31g | Fiber 8.7g | Sugar 5.5g | Protein 9.7g

Parmesan French Fries

Prep Time: 10 minutes.
Cook Time: 20 minutes.
Serves: 6

Ingredients:

- 3 medium russet potatoes
- 2 tablespoons parmesan cheese
- 2 tablespoons fresh parsley, chopped
- 1 tablespoon olive oil
- Salt, to taste

Preparation:

1. At 360 degrees F, preheat your Air Fryer on Air fry mode.
2. Wash the potatoes and pass them through the fries' cutter to get ¼ inch thick fries.
3. Place the fries in a colander and drizzle salt on top.
4. Leave these fries for 10 minutes, then rinse.
5. Toss the potatoes with parmesan cheese, oil, salt, and parsley in a bowl.
6. Place the potatoes into the Air Fryer Basket.
7. Return the Air Fryer Basket to the Air Fryer and cook for 20 minutes.
8. Initiate cooking by pressing the START/PAUSE BUTTON.
9. Toss the chips once cooked halfway through, then resume cooking.
10. Serve warm.

Serving Suggestion: Serve with tomato ketchup, Asian coleslaw, or creamed cabbage.

Variation Tip: Toss fries with black pepper for change of taste.

Nutritional Information Per Serving:
Calories 307 | Fat 8.6g | Sodium 510mg | Carbs 22.2g | Fiber 1.4g | Sugar 13g | Protein 33.6g

Potato Tater Tots

Prep Time: 10 minutes.
Cook Time: 27 minutes.
Serves: 4

Ingredients:

- 2 potatoes, peeled
- 1/2 teaspoons Cajun seasoning
- Olive oil cooking spray
- Sea salt to taste

Preparation:

1. At 375 degrees F, preheat your Air Fryer on Air fry mode.
2. Boil water in a cooking pot and cook potatoes in it for 15 minutes.
3. Drain and leave the potatoes to cool in a bowl.
4. Grate these potatoes and toss them with Cajun seasoning.
5. Make small tater tots out of this mixture.
6. Place them in the Air Fryer Basket and spray them with cooking oil.
7. Return the Air Fryer Basket to the Air Fryer and cook for 27 minutes.
8. Initiate cooking by pressing the START/PAUSE BUTTON.
9. Flip them once cooked halfway through, and resume cooking.
10. Serve warm

Serving Suggestion: Serve with ketchup, mayonnaise, or cream cheese dip.

Variation Tip: Use crushed cornflakes for breading to have extra crispiness.

Nutritional Information Per Serving:
Calories 185 | Fat 11g |Sodium 355mg | Carbs 21g | Fiber 5.8g | Sugar 3g | Protein 4.7g

Chicken Stuffed Mushrooms

Prep Time: 15 minutes.
Cook Time: 15 minutes.
Serves: 6

Ingredients:

- 6 large fresh mushrooms, stems removed
- Stuffing:
- ½ cup chicken meat, cubed
- 1 (4 ounces) package cream cheese, softened
- ¼ lb. imitation crabmeat, flaked
- 1 cup butter
- 1 garlic clove, peeled and minced
- Black pepper and salt to taste
- Garlic powder to taste
- Crushed red pepper to taste

Preparation:

1. At 375 degrees F, preheat your Air Fryer on Air fry mode.
2. Melt and heat butter in a skillet over medium heat.
3. Add chicken and sauté for 5 minutes.
4. Add in all the remaining ingredients for the stuffing.
5. Cook for 5 minutes, then turn off the heat.
6. Allow the mixture to cool. Stuff each mushroom with a tablespoon of this mixture.
7. Place the stuffed mushrooms in the Air Fryer Basket.
8. Return the Air Fryer Basket to the Air Fryer and cook for 15 minutes.
9. Initiate cooking by pressing the START/PAUSE BUTTON.
10. Serve warm.

Serving Suggestion: Serve with mayonnaise or cream cheese dip.

Variation Tip: Use crushed cornflakes for breading to have extra crispiness.

Nutritional Information Per Serving:
Calories 180 | Fat 3.2g |Sodium 133mg | Carbs 32g | Fiber 1.1g | Sugar 1.8g | Protein 9g

Crispy Plantain Chips

Prep Time: 15 minutes.

Cook Time: 20 minutes.

Serves: 4

Ingredients:

- 1 green plantain
- 1 teaspoon canola oil
- 1/2 teaspoons sea salt

Preparation:

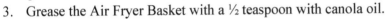

1. At 350 degrees F, preheat your Air Fryer on Air fry mode.
2. Peel and cut the plantains into long strips using a mandolin slicer.
3. Grease the Air Fryer Basket with a ½ teaspoon with canola oil.
4. Toss the plantains with salt and remaining canola oil.
5. Place these plantains in the Air Fryer Basket.
6. Return the Air Fryer Basket to the Air Fryer and cook for 20 minutes.
7. Toss the plantains after 10 minutes and resume cooking.
8. Serve warm.

Serving Suggestion: Serve with cream cheese dip and celery sticks.

Variation Tip: Use black pepper to season the chips.

Nutritional Information Per Serving:

Calories 122 | Fat 1.8g |Sodium 794mg | Carbs 17g | Fiber 8.9g | Sugar 1.6g | Protein 14.9g

Chicken Crescent Wraps

Prep Time: 10 minutes.
Cook Time: 12 minutes.
Serves: 6

Ingredients:

- 3 tablespoons chopped onion
- 3 garlic cloves, peeled and minced
- 3/4 (8 ounces) package cream cheese
- 6 tablespoons butter
- 2 boneless chicken breasts, cubed, cooked
- 3 (10 ounces) cans of refrigerated crescent roll dough

Preparation:

1. At 390 degrees F, preheat your Air Fryer on Air fry mode.
2. Heat oil in a skillet and add onion and garlic to sauté until soft.
3. Add cooked chicken, sautéed veggies, butter, and cream cheese to a blender.
4. Blend well until smooth. Spread the crescent dough over a flat surface.
5. Slice the dough into 12 rectangles.
6. Spoon the chicken mixture at the center of each rectangle.
7. Roll the dough to wrap the mixture and form a ball.
8. Place these balls in the Air Fryer Basket.
9. Return the Air Fryer Basket to the Air Fryer and cook for 12 minutes.
10. Initiate cooking by pressing the START/PAUSE BUTTON.
11. Serve warm

Serving Suggestion: Serve with tomato sauce or cream cheese dip.

Variation Tip: You can also prepare the filling using leftover turkey or pork.

Nutritional Information Per Serving:
Calories 100 | Fat 2g | Sodium 480mg | Carbs 4g | Fiber 2g | Sugar 0g | Protein 18g

Vegetables and Sides Recipes

Curly Fries

Prep Time: 10 minutes.
Cook Time: 20 minutes.
Serves: 6

Ingredients:

- 2 Spiralized Zucchinis
- 1 cup flour
- 2 tbs paprika
- 1 teaspoon cayenne pepper
- 1 teaspoon garlic powder
- 1 teaspoon black pepper
- 1 teaspoon salt
- 2 eggs
- olive oil or cooking spray

Preparation:

1. At 390 degrees F, preheat your Air Fryer on Air fry mode.
2. Mix flour with paprika, cayenne pepper, garlic powder, black pepper, and salt in a bowl.
3. Beat eggs in another bowl and dip the zucchini in the eggs.
4. Coat the zucchini with the flour mixture and place into the Air Fryer Basket.
5. Spray the zucchini with cooking oil.
6. Return the Air Fryer Basket to the Air Fryer and cook for 20 minutes.
7. Initiate cooking by pressing the START/PAUSE BUTTON.
8. Toss the zucchini once cooked halfway through, then resume cooking.
9. Serve warm.

Serving Suggestion: Serve with red chunky salsa or chili sauce.

Variation Tip: Use crushed cornflakes for breading to have extra crispiness.

Nutritional Information Per Serving:
Calories 212 | Fat 11.8g |Sodium 321mg | Carbs 24.6g | Fiber 4.4g | Sugar 8g | Protein 7.3g

Saucy Carrots

Prep Time: 15 minutes.
Cook Time: 25 minutes.
Serves: 6

Ingredients:

- 1 lb. cup carrots, cut into chunks
- 1 tablespoon sesame oil
- ½ tablespoons ginger, minced
- ½ tablespoons soy sauce
- ½ teaspoon garlic, minced
- ½ tablespoons scallions, chopped, for garnish
- ½ teaspoon sesame seeds for garnish

Preparation:

1. At 390 degrees F, preheat your Air Fryer on Air fry mode.
2. Toss all the ginger carrots ingredients, except the sesame seeds and scallions, in a suitable bowl.
3. Place the carrots in the Air Fryer Basket in a single layer.
4. Return the Air Fryer Basket to the Air Fryer and cook for 25 minutes.
5. Initiate cooking by pressing the START/PAUSE BUTTON.
6. Toss the carrots once cooked halfway through.
7. Garnish with sesame seeds and scallions.
8. Serve warm

Serving Suggestion: Serve with mayo sauce or ketchup.

Variation Tip: Use some honey for a sweet taste.

Nutritional Information Per Serving:

Calories 206 | Fat 3.4g | Sodium 174mg | Carbs 35g | Fiber 9.4g | Sugar 5.9g | Protein 10.6g

Fried Artichoke Hearts

Prep Time: 15 minutes.
Cook Time: 10 minutes.
Serves: 6

Ingredients:

- 3 cans Quartered Artichokes, drained
- 1/2 cup mayonnaise
- 1 cup panko breadcrumbs
- ⅓ cup grated Parmesan
- salt and black pepper to taste
- Parsley for garnish

Preparation:

1. At 375 degrees F, preheat your Air Fryer on Air fry mode.
2. Mix mayonnaise with salt and black pepper and keep the sauce aside.
3. Spread panko breadcrumbs in a bowl.
4. Coat the artichoke pieces with the breadcrumbs.
5. As you coat the artichokes, place them in the Air Fryer Basket in a single layer, then spray them with cooking oil.
6. Return the Air Fryer Basket to the Air Fryer and cook for 10 minutes.
7. Initiate cooking by pressing the START/PAUSE BUTTON.
8. Flip the artichokes once cooked halfway through, then resume cooking.
9. Serve warm with mayo sauce.

Serving Suggestion: Serve with red chunky salsa or chili sauce.

Variation Tip: Use crushed cornflakes for breading to have extra crispiness.

Nutritional Information Per Serving:
Calories 193 | Fat 1g |Sodium 395mg | Carbs 38.7g | Fiber 1.6g | Sugar 0.9g | Protein 6.6g

Fried Olives

Prep Time: 15 minutes.

Cook Time: 9 minutes.

Serves: 6

Ingredients:

- 2 cups blue cheese stuffed olives, drained
- 1/2 cup all-purpose flour
- 1 cup panko breadcrumbs
- 1/2 teaspoons garlic powder
- 1 pinch of oregano
- 2 eggs

Preparation:

1. At 375 degrees F, preheat your Air Fryer on Air fry mode.
2. Mix flour with oregano and garlic powder in a bowl and beat two eggs in another bowl.
3. Spread panko breadcrumbs in a bowl.
4. Coat all the olives with the flour mixture, dip in the eggs and then coat with the panko breadcrumbs.
5. As you coat the olives, place them in the Air Fryer Basket in a single layer, then spray them with cooking oil.
6. Return the Air Fryer Basket to the Air Fryer and cook for 9 minutes.
7. Initiate cooking by pressing the START/PAUSE BUTTON.
8. Flip the olives once cooked halfway through, then resume cooking.
9. Serve.

Serving Suggestion: Serve with red chunky salsa or chili sauce.

Variation Tip: Use crushed cornflakes for breading to have extra crispiness.

Nutritional Information Per Serving:

Calories 166 | Fat 3.2g |Sodium 437mg | Carbs 28.8g | Fiber 1.8g | Sugar 2.7g | Protein 5.8g

Falafel

Prep Time: 15 minutes.

Cook Time: 14 minutes.

Serves: 6

Ingredients:

- 1 (15.5 oz) can chickpeas, rinsed and drained
- 1 small yellow onion, cut into quarters
- 3 garlic cloves, chopped
- 1/3 cup parsley, chopped
- 1/3 cup cilantro, chopped
- 1/3 cup scallions, chopped
- 1 teaspoon cumin
- 1/2 teaspoons salt
- 1/8 teaspoons crushed red pepper flakes
- 1 teaspoon baking powder
- 4 tablespoons all-purpose flour
- Olive oil spray

Preparation:

1. At 350 degrees F, preheat your Air Fryer on Air fry mode.
2. Dry the chickpeas on paper towels.
3. Add onions and garlic to a food processor and chop them.
4. Add the parsley, salt, cilantro, scallions, cumin, and red pepper flakes.
5. Press the pulse button for 60 seconds, then toss in chickpeas and blend for 3 times until it makes a chunky paste.
6. Stir in baking powder and flour and mix well.
7. Transfer the falafel mixture to a bowl and cover to refrigerate for 3 hours.
8. Make 12 balls out of the falafel mixture.
9. Place falafels in the Air Fryer Basket and spray them with oil.
10. Return the Air Fryer Basket to the Air Fryer and cook for 14 minutes.
11. Initiate cooking by pressing the START/PAUSE BUTTON.
12. Toss the falafel once cooked halfway through, and resume cooking.
13. Serve warm

Serving Suggestion: Serve with yogurt dip and sautéed carrots.

Variation Tip: Use breadcrumbs for breading to have extra crispiness.

Nutritional Information Per Serving:

Calories 113 | Fat 3g |Sodium 152mg | Carbs 20g | Fiber 3g | Sugar 1.1g | Protein 3.5g

Quinoa Patties

Prep Time: 15 minutes.
Cook Time: 32 minutes.
Serves: 4

Ingredients:

- 1 cup quinoa red
- 1½ cups water
- 1 teaspoon salt
- black pepper, ground
- 1½ cups rolled oats
- 3 eggs beaten
- ¼ cup minced white onion
- ½ cup crumbled feta cheese
- ¼ cup chopped fresh chives
- Salt and black pepper, to taste
- Vegetable or canola oil
- 4 hamburger buns
- 4 arugulas
- 4 slices tomato sliced

Cucumber yogurt dill sauce

- 1 cup cucumber, diced
- 1 cup Greek yogurt
- 2 teaspoons lemon juice
- ¼ teaspoons salt
- Black pepper, ground
- 1 tablespoon chopped fresh dill
- 1 tablespoon olive oil

Preparation:

1. At 390 degrees F, preheat your Air Fryer on Air fry mode.
2. Add quinoa to a saucepan filled with cold water, salt, and black pepper, and place it over medium-high heat.
3. Cook the quinoa to a boil, then reduce the heat, cover, and cook for 20 minutes on a simmer.
4. Fluff and mix the cooked quinoa with a fork and remove it from the heat.
5. Spread the quinoa in a baking stay.
6. Mix eggs, oats, onion, herbs, cheese, salt, and black pepper.
7. Stir in quinoa, then mix well. Make 4 patties out of this quinoa cheese mixture.
8. Place the patties in the Air Fryer Basket and spray them with cooking oil.
9. Return the Air Fryer Basket to the Air Fryer and cook for 13 minutes.
10. Initiate cooking by pressing the START/PAUSE BUTTON.
11. Flip the patties once cooked halfway through, and resume cooking.
12. Meanwhile, prepare the cucumber yogurt dill sauce by mixing all of its ingredients in a mixing bowl.
13. Place each quinoa patty in a burger bun along with arugula leaves.
14. Serve with yogurt dill sauce.

Serving Suggestion: Serve with yogurt dip.

Variation Tip: Use crushed cornflakes for breading to have extra crispiness.

Nutritional Information Per Serving:
Calories 231 | Fat 9g |Sodium 271mg | Carbs 32.8g | Fiber 6.4g | Sugar 7g | Protein 6.3g

Lime Glazed Tofu

Prep Time: 10 minutes.
Cook Time: 14 minutes.
Serves: 6

Ingredients:

- ⅔ cup coconut aminos
- 2 (14 oz) packages extra-firm, water-packed tofu, drained
- 6 tablespoons toasted sesame oil
- ⅔ cup lime juice

Preparation:

1. At 400 degrees F, preheat your Air Fryer on Air fry mode.
2. Pat dry the tofu bars and slice into half-inch cubes.
3. Toss all the remaining ingredients in a small bowl.
4. Marinate for 4 hours in the refrigerator. Drain off the excess water.
5. Place the tofu cubes in the Air Fryer Basket.
6. Return the Air Fryer Basket to the Air Fryer and cook for 14 minutes.
7. Initiate cooking by pressing the START/PAUSE BUTTON.
8. Toss the tofu once cooked halfway through, then resume cooking.
9. Serve warm

Serving Suggestion: Serve with sautéed green vegetables.

Variation Tip: Add sautéed onion and carrot to the tofu cubes.

Nutritional Information Per Serving:
Calories 284 | Fat 7.9g | Sodium 704mg | Carbs 38.1g | Fiber 1.9g | Sugar 1.9g | Protein 14.8g

Sweet Potatoes with Honey Butter

Prep Time: 15 minutes.
Cook Time: 40 minutes.
Serves: 4

Ingredients:

- 4 sweet potatoes, scrubbed
- 1 teaspoon oil

Honey Butter

- 4 tablespoons unsalted butter
- 1 tablespoon Honey
- 2 teaspoons hot sauce
- ¼ teaspoons salt

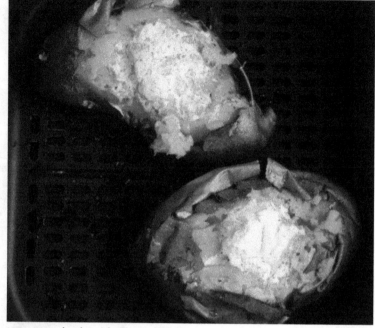

Preparation:

1. At 390 degrees F, preheat your Air Fryer on Air fry mode.
2. Rub the sweet potatoes with oil and place two potatoes in the Air Fryer Basket.
3. Return the Air Fryer Basket to the Air Fryer and cook for 40 minutes.
4. Initiate cooking by pressing the START/PAUSE BUTTON.
5. Flip the potatoes once cooked halfway through, then resume cooking.
6. Mix butter with hot sauce, honey, and salt in a bowl.
7. When the potatoes are done, cut a slit on top and make a well with a spoon
8. Pour the honey butter into each potato jacket.
9. Serve.

Serving Suggestion: Serve with sautéed vegetables and salad.

Variation Tip: Sprinkle crumbled bacon and parsley on top.

Nutritional Information Per Serving:

Calories 288 | Fat 6.9g | Sodium 761mg | Carbs 46g | Fiber 4g | Sugar 12g | Protein 9.6g

Hasselback Potatoes

Prep Time: 15 minutes.

Cook Time: 15 minutes.

Serves: 4

Ingredients:

- 4 medium Yukon Gold potatoes
- 3 tablespoons melted butter
- 1 tablespoon olive oil
- 3 garlic cloves, crushed
- ½ teaspoon ground paprika
- Salt and black pepper ground, to taste
- 1 tablespoon chopped fresh parsley

Preparation:

1. At 375 degrees F, preheat your Air Fryer on Air fry mode.
2. Slice each potato from the top to make 1/4-inch slices without cutting its 1/2-inch bottom, keeping the potato's bottom intact.
3. Mix butter with olive oil, garlic, and paprika in a small bowl.
4. Brush the garlic mixture on top of each potato and add the mixture into the slits.
5. Season them with salt and black pepper.
6. Place the seasoned potatoes in the Air Fryer Basket
7. Return the Air Fryer Basket to the Air Fryer and cook for 25 minutes.
8. Initiate cooking by pressing the START/PAUSE BUTTON.
9. Brushing the potatoes again with butter mixture after 15 minutes, then resume cooking.
10. Garnish with parsley.
11. Serve warm

Serving Suggestion: Serve with mayonnaise or cream cheese dip.

Variation Tip: Add tomato and cheese slices to the potato slits before air frying.

Nutritional Information Per Serving:

Calories 350 | Fat 2.6g |Sodium 358mg | Carbs 64.6g | Fiber 14.4g | Sugar 3.3g | Protein 19.9g

Zucchini Cakes

Prep Time: 10 minutes.
Cook Time: 32 minutes.
Serves: 6

Ingredients:

- 2 medium zucchinis, grated
- 1 cup corn kernel
- 1 medium potato cooked
- 2 tablespoons chickpea flour
- 2 garlic minced
- 2 teaspoons olive oil
- Salt and black pepper
- For Serving:
- Yogurt tahini sauce

Preparation:

1. At 390 degrees F, preheat your Air Fryer on Air fry mode.
2. Mix grated zucchini with a pinch of salt in a colander and leave them for 15 minutes.
3. Squeeze out their excess water.
4. Mash the cooked potato in a large-sized bowl with a fork.
5. Add zucchini, corn, garlic, chickpea flour, salt, and black pepper to the bowl.
6. Mix these fritters' ingredients together and make 2 tablespoons-sized balls out of this mixture and flatten them lightly.
7. Place the fritters in the Air Fryer Basket in a single layer and spray them with cooking.
8. Return the Air Fryer Basket to the Air Fryer and cook for 17 minutes.
9. Initiate cooking by pressing the START/PAUSE BUTTON.
10. Flip the fritters once cooked halfway through, then resume cooking.
11. Serve

Serving Suggestion: Serve with mayonnaise or cream cheese dip.

Variation Tip: Use crushed cornflakes for breading to have extra crispiness.

Nutritional Information Per Serving:

Calories 270 | Fat 14.6g |Sodium 394mg | Carbs 31.3g | Fiber 7.5g | Sugar 9.7g | Protein 6.4g

Air Fried Okra

Prep Time: 10 minutes.

Cook Time: 13 minutes.

Serves: 2

Ingredients:

- ½ lb okra pods sliced
- 1 teaspoon olive oil
- ¼ teaspoons salt
- ⅛ teaspoons black pepper

Preparation:

1. At 375 degrees F, preheat your Air Fryer on Air fry mode.
2. Toss okra with olive oil, salt, and black pepper in a bowl.
3. Spread the okra in a single layer in the Air Fryer Basket.
4. Return the Air Fryer Basket to the Air Fryer and cook for 13 minutes.
5. Initiate cooking by pressing the START/PAUSE BUTTON.
6. Toss the okra once cooked halfway through, and resume cooking.
7. Serve warm

Serving Suggestion: Serve with potato chips and bread slices.

Variation Tip: Sprinkle cornmeal before cooking for added crispiness.

Nutritional Information Per Serving:

Calories 208 | Fat 5g |Sodium 1205mg | Carbs 34.1g | Fiber 7.8g | Sugar 2.5g | Protein 5.9g

Fish and Seafood Recipes

Salmon Nuggets

Prep Time: 15 minutes.
Cook Time: 15 minutes.
Serves: 4

Ingredients:

- ⅓ cup maple syrup
- ¼ teaspoon dried chipotle pepper
- 1 pinch sea salt
- 1 ½ cups croutons
- 1 large egg
- 1 (1 pound) skinless salmon fillet, cut into
1 1/2-inch chunk
- cooking spray

Preparation:

1. At 390 degrees F, preheat your Air Fryer on Air fry mode.
2. Mix chipotle powder, maple syrup, and salt in a saucepan and cook on a simmer for 5 minutes.
3. Crush the croutons in a food processor and transfer them to a bowl.
4. Beat egg in another shallow bowl.
5. Season the salmon chunks with sea salt.
6. Dip the salmon in the egg, then coat with breadcrumbs.
7. Spread the coated salmon chunks in the Air Fryer Basket.
8. Return the Air Fryer Basket to the Air Fryer and cook for 10 minutes.
9. Initiate cooking by pressing the START/PAUSE BUTTON.
10. Flip the chunks once cooked halfway through, then resume cooking.
11. Pour the maple syrup on top and serve warm.

Serving Suggestion: Serve with creamy dip and crispy fries.

Variation Tip: Use crushed cornflakes for breading to have extra crispiness.

Nutritional Information Per Serving:
Calories 275 | Fat 1.4g |Sodium 582mg | Carbs 31.5g | Fiber 1.1g | Sugar 0.1g | Protein 29.8g

Fish Sandwich

Prep Time: 15 minutes.

Cook Time: 22 minutes.

Serves: 4

Ingredients:

- 4 small cod fillets, skinless
- Salt and black pepper, to taste
- 2 tablespoons flour
- ¼ cup dried breadcrumbs
- Spray oil
- 9 ounces of frozen peas
- 1 tablespoon creme fraiche
- 12 capers
- 1 squeeze of lemon juice
- 4 bread rolls, cut in halve

Preparation:

1. At 390 degrees F, preheat your Air Fryer on Air fry mode.
2. First, coat the cod fillets with flour, salt, and black pepper.
3. Then coat the fish with breadcrumbs.
4. Place the coated codfish in the Air Fryer Basket and spray them with cooking spray.
5. Return the Air Fryer Basket to the Air Fryer and cook for 17 minutes.
6. Initiate cooking by pressing the START/PAUSE BUTTON.
7. Meanwhile, boil peas in hot water for 5 minutes until soft.
8. Then drain the peas and transfer them to the blender.
9. Add capers, lemon juice, and crème fraiche to the blender.
10. Blend until it makes a smooth mixture.
11. Spread the peas crème mixture on top of 2 lower halves of the bread roll, and place the fish fillets on it.
12. Place the remaining bread slices on top.
13. Serve fresh

Serving Suggestion: Serve with sautéed or fresh greens with melted butter.

Variation Tip: Coat the fish with crushed cornflakes for extra crispiness.

Nutritional Information Per Serving:

Calories 348 | Fat 30g |Sodium 660mg | Carbs 5g | Fiber 0g | Sugar 0g | Protein 14g

Breaded Scallops

Prep Time: 15 minutes.
Cook Time: 12 minutes.
Serves: 4

Ingredients:

- ½ cup crushed buttery crackers
- ½ teaspoon garlic powder
- ½ teaspoon seafood seasoning
- 2 tablespoons butter, melted
- 1-pound sea scallops patted dry
- cooking spray

Preparation:

1. At 390 degrees F, preheat your Air Fryer on Air fry mode.
2. Mix cracker crumbs, garlic powder, and seafood seasoning in a shallow bowl. Spread melted butter in another shallow bowl.
3. Dip each scallop in the melted butter and then roll in the breading to coat well.
4. Grease the Air Fryer Basket with cooking spray and place the scallops inside.
5. Return the Air Fryer Basket to the Air Fryer and cook for 12 minutes.
6. Initiate cooking by pressing the START/PAUSE BUTTON.
7. Flip the scallops with a spatula after 4 minutes and resume cooking.
8. Serve warm.

Serving Suggestion: Serve with creamy dip and crispy fries.

Variation Tip: Use crushed cornflakes for breading to have extra crispiness.

Nutritional Information Per Serving:
Calories 275 | Fat 1.4g |Sodium 582mg | Carbs 31.5g | Fiber 1.1g | Sugar 0.1g | Protein 29.8g

Fried Lobster Tails

Prep Time: 10 minutes.

Cook Time: 18 minutes.

Serves: 4

Ingredients:

- 4 (4 oz) lobster tails
- 8 tablespoons butter, melted
- 2 teaspoons lemon zest
- 2 garlic cloves, grated
- Salt and black pepper ground to taste
- 2 teaspoons fresh parsley, chopped
- 4 wedges lemon

Preparation:

1. At 350 degrees F, preheat your Air Fryer on Air fry mode.
2. Spread the lobster tails into Butterfly, slit the top to expose the lobster meat while keeping the tail intact.
3. Place the lobster tails in the Air Fryer Basket with their lobster meat facing up.
4. Mix melted butter with lemon zest and garlic in a bowl.
5. Brush the butter mixture on top of the lobster tails.
6. And drizzle salt and black pepper on top.
7. Return the Air Fryer Basket to the Air Fryer and cook for 18 minutes.
8. Initiate cooking by pressing the START/PAUSE BUTTON.
9. Garnish with parsley and lemon wedges.
10. Serve warm

Serving Suggestion: Serve on a bed of lettuce leaves.

Variation Tip: Drizzle crushed cornflakes on top to have extra crispiness.

Nutritional Information Per Serving:

Calories 257 | Fat 10.4g |Sodium 431mg | Carbs 20g | Fiber 0g | Sugar 1.6g | Protein 21g

Salmon Patties

Prep Time: 15 minutes.
Cook Time: 18 minutes.
Serves: 8

Ingredients:

- 1 lb fresh Atlantic salmon side
- 1/4 cup avocado, mashed
- 1/4 cup cilantro, diced
- 1 1/2 teaspoons yellow curry powder
- 1/2 teaspoons sea salt
- 1/4 cup, 4 teaspoons tapioca starch
- 2 brown eggs
- 1/2 cup coconut flakes
- Coconut oil, melted, for brushing
- For the greens:
- 2 teaspoons organic coconut oil, melted
- 6 cups arugula & spinach mix, tightly packed
- Pinch of sea salt

Preparation:

1. At 390 degrees F, preheat your Air Fryer on Air fry mode.
2. Remove the fish skin and dice the flesh.
3. Place in a large bowl. Add cilantro, avocado, salt, and curry powder mix gently.
4. Add tapioca starch and mix well again.
5. Make 8 salmon patties out of this mixture, about a half-inch thick.
6. Place them on a baking sheet lined with wax paper and freeze them for 20 minutes.
7. Place ¼ cup tapioca starch and coconut flakes on a flat plate.
8. Dip the patties in the whisked egg, then coat the frozen patties in the starch and flakes.
9. Place the patties in the Air Fryer Basket and spray them with cooking oil
10. Return the Air Fryer Basket to the Air Fryer and cook for 17 minutes.
11. Initiate cooking by pressing the START/PAUSE BUTTON.
12. Flip the patties once cooked halfway through, then resume cooking.
13. Sauté arugula with spinach in coconut oil in a pan for 30 seconds.
14. Serve the patties with sautéed greens mixture

Serving Suggestion: Serve with sautéed green beans or asparagus.

Variation Tip: Add lemon juice to the mixture before mixing.

Nutritional Information Per Serving:
Calories 260 | Fat 16g |Sodium 585mg | Carbs 3.1g | Fiber 1.3g | Sugar 0.2g | Protein 25.5g

Glazed Scallops

Prep Time: 15 minutes.

Cook Time: 13 minutes.

Serves: 6

Ingredients:

- 12 scallops
- 3 tablespoons olive oil
- Black pepper and salt to taste

Preparation:

1. At 390 degrees F, preheat your Air Fryer on Air fry mode.
2. Rub the scallops with olive oil, black pepper, and salt.
3. Place the scallops in the Air Fryer Basket.
4. Return the Air Fryer Basket to the Air Fryer and cook for 13 minutes.
5. Initiate cooking by pressing the START/PAUSE BUTTON.
6. Flip the scallops once cooked halfway through, and resume cooking.
7. Serve warm

Serving Suggestion: Serve with melted butter on top.

Variation Tip: Drizzle breadcrumbs on top before Air Frying.

Nutritional Information Per Serving:

Calories 308 | Fat 24g |Sodium 715mg | Carbs 0.8g | Fiber 0.1g | Sugar 0.1g | Protein 21.9g

Salmon with Fennel Salad

Prep Time: 10 minutes.
Cook Time: 17 minutes.
Serves: 4

Ingredients:

- 2 teaspoons fresh parsley, chopped
- 1 teaspoon fresh thyme, chopped
- 1 teaspoon salt
- 4 (6-oz) skinless center-cut salmon fillets
- 2 tablespoons olive oil
- 4 cups fennel, sliced
- 2/3 cup Greek yogurt
- 1 garlic clove, grated
- 2 tablespoons orange juice
- 1 teaspoon lemon juice
- 2 tablespoons fresh dill, chopped

Preparation:

1. At 390 degrees F, preheat your Air Fryer on Air fry mode.
2. Mix ½ teaspoon salt, thyme, and parsley in a small bowl.
3. Brush the salmon with oil first, then rub liberally rub the herb mixture.
4. Place salmon fillets in the Air Fryer Basket.
5. Return the Air Fryer Basket to the Air Fryer and cook for 17 minutes.
6. Initiate cooking by pressing the START/PAUSE BUTTON.
7. Meanwhile, mix fennel with garlic, yogurt, lemon juice, orange juice, remaining salt, and dill in a mixing bowl.
8. Serve the Air Fried Salmon fillets with fennel salad.
9. Enjoy.

Serving Suggestion: Serve with melted butter on top.

Variation Tip: Rub the salmon with lemon juice before cooking.

Nutritional Information Per Serving:
Calories 305 | Fat 15g |Sodium 482mg | Carbs 17g | Fiber 3g | Sugar 2g | Protein 35g

Crusted Tilapia

Prep Time: 20 minutes.

Cook Time: 17 minutes.

Serves: 4

Ingredients:

- 3/4 cup breadcrumbs
- 1 packet dry ranch-style dressing
- 2 1/2 tablespoons vegetable oil
- 2 eggs beaten
- 4 tilapia fillets
- Herbs and chilies to garnish

Preparation:

1. At 390 degrees F, preheat your Air Fryer on Air fry mode.
2. Thoroughly mix ranch dressing with panko in a bowl.
3. Whisk eggs in a shallow bowl.
4. Dip each fish fillet in the egg, then coat evenly with the panko mixture.
5. Set two coated fillets in the Air Fryer Basket.
6. Return the Air Fryer Basket to the Air Fryer and cook for 17 minutes.
7. Initiate cooking by pressing the START/PAUSE BUTTON.
8. Serve warm with herbs and chilies

Serving Suggestion: Serve with sautéed asparagus on the side.

Variation Tip: Coat the fish with crushed cornflakes for extra crispiness.

Nutritional Information Per Serving:

Calories 196 | Fat 7.1g |Sodium 492mg | Carbs 21.6g | Fiber 2.9g | Sugar 0.8g | Protein 13.4g

Scallops with Greens

Prep Time: 15 minutes.
Cook Time: 13 minutes.
Serves: 8

Ingredients:

- 3/4 cup heavy whipping cream
- 1 tablespoon tomato paste
- 1 tablespoon chopped fresh basil
- 1 teaspoon garlic, minced
- 1/2 teaspoons salt
- 1/2 teaspoons pepper
- 12 ounces frozen spinach thawed
- 8 jumbo sea scallops
- Vegetable oil to spray

Preparation:

1. At 390 degrees F, preheat your Air Fryer on Air fry mode.
2. Season the scallops with vegetable oil, salt, and pepper in a bowl
3. Mix cream with spinach, basil, garlic, salt, pepper, and tomato paste in a bowl.
4. Pour this mixture over the scallops and mix gently.
5. Place the scallops in the Air Fryers Basket without using the crisper plate.
6. Return the Air Fryer Basket to the Air Fryer and cook for 13 minutes.
7. Initiate cooking by pressing the START/PAUSE BUTTON.
8. Serve right away

Serving Suggestion: Serve with fresh cucumber salad.

Variation Tip: Use crushed cornflakes for breading to have extra crispiness.

Nutritional Information Per Serving:
Calories 266 | Fat 6.3g |Sodium 193mg | Carbs 39.1g | Fiber 7.2g | Sugar 5.2g | Protein 14.8g

Crusted Cod

Prep Time: 15 minutes.

Cook Time: 13 minutes.

Serves: 4

Ingredients:

- 2 lbs cod fillets
- Salt, to taste
- Freshly black pepper, to taste
- ½ cup all-purpose flour
- 1 large egg, beaten
- 2 cups panko bread crumbs
- 1 teaspoon Old Bay seasoning
- Lemon wedges, for serving
- Tartar sauce, for serving

Preparation:

1. At 390 degrees F, preheat your Air Fryer on Air fry mode.
2. Rub the fish with salt and black pepper.
3. Add flour in one shallow bowl, beat eggs in another bowl, and mix panko with Old Bay in a shallow bowl.
4. First, coat the fish with flour, then dip it in the eggs and finally coat it with the panko mixture.
5. Place the seasoned codfish in the Air Fryer Basket.
6. Return the Air Fryer Basket to the Air Fryer and cook for 13 minutes.
7. Initiate cooking by pressing the START/PAUSE BUTTON.
8. Flip the fish once cooked halfway, then resume cooking.
9. Serve warm and fresh with tartar sauce and lemon wedges.

Serving Suggestion: Enjoy with creamy coleslaw on the side.

Variation Tip: Use crushed cornflakes for extra crispiness.

Nutritional Information Per Serving:

Calories 155 | Fat 4.2g |Sodium 963mg | Carbs 21.5g | Fiber 0.8g | Sugar 5.7g | Protein 8.1g

Buttered Mahi Mahi

Prep Time: 15 minutes.
Cook Time: 22 minutes.
Serves: 4

Ingredients:

- 4 (6 oz) mahi-mahi fillets
- Salt and black pepper ground to taste
- Cooking spray
- ⅔ cup butter

Preparation:

1. At 390 degrees F, preheat your Air Fryer on Air fry mode.
2. Rub the Mahi-mahi fillets with salt and black pepper.
3. Place mahi-mahi fillets in the Air Fryer's Basket.
4. Return the Air Fryer Basket to the Air Fryer and cook for 17 minutes.
5. Initiate cooking by pressing the START/PAUSE BUTTON.
6. Add butter to a saucepan and cook for 5 minutes until slightly brown.
7. Remove the butter from the heat.
8. Drizzle butter over the fish and serve warm.

Serving Suggestion: Serve with pasta or fried rice.

Variation Tip: Drizzle parmesan cheese on top.

Nutritional Information Per Serving:
Calories 399 | Fat 16g |Sodium 537mg | Carbs 28g | Fiber 3g | Sugar 10g | Protein 35g

Crusted Shrimp

Prep Time: 20 minutes.

Cook Time: 13 minutes.

Serves: 4

Ingredients:

- 1 lb shrimp
- 1/2 cup flour, all-purpose
- 1 teaspoon salt
- 1/2 teaspoons baking powder
- 2/3 cup water
- 2 cups coconut shred
- 1/2 cup bread crumbs

Preparation:

1. At 390 degrees F, preheat your Air Fryer on Air fry mode.
2. In a small bowl, whisk together flour, salt, water, and baking powder. Set aside for 5 minutes.
3. In another shallow bowl, toss bread crumbs with coconut shreds together.
4. Dredge shrimp in liquid, then coat in coconut mixture, making sure it's totally covered.
5. Repeat until all shrimp are coated.
6. Spread the shrimp in the Air Fryer Basket and spray them with cooking oil.
7. Return the Air Fryer Basket to the Air Fryer and cook for 13 minutes.
8. Initiate cooking by pressing the START/PAUSE BUTTON.
9. Shake the basket once cooked halfway, then resume cooking.
10. Serve with your favorite dip.

Serving Suggestion: Serve on top of mashed potato or mashed cauliflower.

Variation Tip: Use crushed cornflakes for breading to have extra crispiness.

Nutritional Information Per Serving:

Calories 297 | Fat 1g |Sodium 291mg | Carbs 35g | Fiber 1g | Sugar 9g | Protein 29g

Crispy Catfish

Prep Time: 15 minutes.
Cook Time: 17 minutes.
Serves: 4

Ingredients:

- 4 catfish fillets
- 1/4 cup Louisiana Fish fry
- 1 tablespoon olive oil
- 1 tablespoon parsley, chopped
- 1 lemon, sliced
- Fresh herbs to garnish

Preparation:

1. At 390 degrees F, preheat your Air Fryer on Air fry mode.
2. Mix fish fry with olive oil, and parsley then liberally rub over the catfish.
3. Place two fillets in the Air Fryer Basket.
4. Return the Air Fryer Basket to the Air Fryer and cook for 17 minutes.
5. Initiate cooking by pressing the START/PAUSE BUTTON.
6. Garnish with lemon slices and herbs.
7. Serve warm

Serving Suggestion: Serve with creamy dip and crispy fries.

Variation Tip: Use crushed cornflakes for breading to have extra crispiness.

Nutritional Information Per Serving:

Calories 275 | Fat 1.4g |Sodium 582mg | Carbs 31.5g | Fiber 1.1g | Sugar 0.1g | Protein 29.8g

Savory Salmon Fillets

Prep Time: 10 minutes.
Cook Time: 17 minutes.
Serves: 4

Ingredients:

- 4 (6-oz) salmon fillets
- Salt, to taste
- Black pepper, to taste
- 4 teaspoons olive oil
- 4 tablespoons wholegrain mustard
- 2 tablespoons packed brown sugar
- 2 garlic cloves, minced
- 1 teaspoon thyme leaves

Preparation:

1. At 390 degrees F, preheat your Air Fryer on Air fry mode.
2. Rub the salmon with salt and black pepper first.
3. Whisk oil with sugar, thyme, garlic, and mustard in a small bowl.
4. Place salmon fillets in the Air Fryer Basket and brush the thyme mixture on top of each fillet.
5. Return the Air Fryer Basket to the Air Fryer and cook for 17 minutes.
6. Initiate cooking by pressing the START/PAUSE BUTTON.
7. Serve warm and fresh

Serving Suggestion: Serve with parsley and melted butter on top.

Variation Tip: Rub the fish fillets with lemon juice before cooking.

Nutritional Information Per Serving:
Calories 336 | Fat 6g |Sodium 181mg | Carbs 1.3g | Fiber 0.2g | Sugar 0.4g | Protein 69.2g

Poultry Mains Recipes

Crumbed Chicken Katsu

Prep Time: 15 minutes.
Cook Time: 26 minutes.
Serves: 4

Ingredients:

- 1 lb boneless chicken breast, cut in half
- 2 large eggs, beaten
- 1 ½ cups panko bread crumbs
- Salt and black pepper ground to taste
- Cooking spray

Sauce:

- 1 tablespoon sugar
- 2 tablespoons soy sauce
- 1 tablespoon sherry
- ½ cup ketchup
- 2 teaspoons Worcestershire sauce
- 1 teaspoon garlic, minced

Preparation:

1. At 390 degrees F, preheat your Air Fryer on Air fry mode.
2. Mix soy sauce, ketchup, sherry, sugar, garlic, and Worcestershire sauce in a mixing bowl.
3. Keep this katsu aside for a while.
4. Rub the chicken pieces with salt and black pepper.
5. Whisk eggs in a shallow dish and spread breadcrumbs in another tray.
6. Dip the chicken in the egg mixture and coat them with breadcrumbs.
7. Place the coated chicken in the Air Fryer Basket and spray them with cooking spray.
8. Return the Air Fryer Basket to the Air Fryer and cook for 26 minutes.
9. Initiate cooking by pressing the START/PAUSE BUTTON.
10. Flip the chicken once cooked halfway through, then resume cooking.
11. Serve warm with the sauce

Serving Suggestion: Serve with fried rice and green beans salad.

Variation Tip: Coat the chicken with crushed cornflakes for extra crispiness.

Nutritional Information Per Serving:
Calories 220 | Fat 1.7g |Sodium 178mg | Carbs 1.7g | Fiber 0.2g | Sugar 0.2g | Protein 32.9g

Pickled Chicken Fillets

Prep Time: 15 minutes.
Cook Time: 28 minutes.
Serves: 4

Ingredients:

- 2 boneless chicken breasts
- 1/2 cup dill pickle juice
- 2 eggs
- 1/2 cup milk
- 1 cup flour, all-purpose
- 2 tablespoons powdered sugar
- 2 tablespoons potato starch
- 1 teaspoon paprika
- 1 teaspoon of sea salt
- 1/2 teaspoons black pepper
- 1/2 teaspoons garlic powder
- 1/4 teaspoons ground celery seed ground
- 1 tablespoon olive oil

- Cooking spray
- 4 hamburger buns, toasted
- 8 dill pickle chips

Preparation:

1. At 390 degrees F, preheat your Air Fryer on Air fry mode.
2. Set the chicken in a suitable Ziplock bag and pound it into ½ thickness with a mallet.
3. Slice the chicken into 2 halves.
4. Add pickle juice and seal the bag.
5. Refrigerate for 30 minutes approximately for marination. Whisk both eggs with milk in a shallow bowl.
6. Thoroughly mix flour with spices and flour in a separate bowl.
7. Dip each chicken slice in egg, then in the flour mixture.
8. Shake off the excess and set the chicken pieces in the Air Fryer Basket.
9. Spray the pieces with cooking oil.
10. Place the chicken pieces in the Air Fryer Basket in a single layer and spray the cooking oil.
11. Return the Air Fryer Basket to the Air Fryer and cook for 28 minutes.
12. Initiate cooking by pressing the START/PAUSE BUTTON.
13. Flip the chicken pieces once cooked halfway through, and resume cooking.
14. Enjoy with pickle chips and a dollop of mayonnaise.

Serving Suggestion: Serve with warm corn tortilla and Greek salad.

Variation Tip: You can use the almond flour breading for a low-carb serving.

Nutritional Information Per Serving:
Calories 353 | Fat 5g |Sodium 818mg | Carbs 53.2g | Fiber 4.4g | Sugar 8g | Protein 17.3g

Crusted Chicken Breast

Prep Time: 15 minutes.
Cook Time: 28 minutes.
Serves: 4

Ingredients:

- 2 large eggs, beaten
- 1/2 cup all-purpose flour
- 1 1/4 cup panko bread crumbs
- 2/3 cup Parmesan, grated
- 4 teaspoons lemon zest
- 2 teaspoons dried oregano
- Salt, to taste
- 1 teaspoon cayenne pepper
- Freshly black pepper, to taste
- 4 boneless skinless chicken breasts

Preparation:

1. At 390 degrees F, preheat your Air Fryer on Air fry mode.
2. Beat eggs in one shallow bowl and spread flour in another shallow bowl.
3. Mix panko with oregano, lemon zest, Parmesan, cayenne, oregano, salt, and black pepper in another shallow bowl.
4. First, coat the chicken with flour first, then dip it in the eggs and coat them with panko mixture.
5. Arrange the prepared chicken in the Air Fryer Basket.
6. Return the Air Fryer Basket to the Air Fryer and cook for 28 minutes.
7. Initiate cooking by pressing the START/PAUSE BUTTON.
8. Flip the half-cooked chicken and continue cooking until golden.
9. Serve warm

Serving Suggestion: Serve with fresh-cut tomatoes and sautéed greens.

Variation Tip: Rub the chicken with lemon juice before seasoning.

Nutritional Information Per Serving:
Calories 220 | Fat 13g |Sodium 542mg | Carbs 0.9g | Fiber 0.3g | Sugar 0.2g | Protein 25.6g

Chili Chicken Wings

Prep Time: 20 minutes.
Cook Time: 43 minutes.
Serves: 4

Ingredients:

- 8 chicken wings drumettes
- cooking spray
- 1/8 cup low-fat buttermilk
- 1/4 cup almond flour
- McCormick Chicken Seasoning to taste

Thai Chili Marinade

- 1 1/2 tablespoons low-sodium soy sauce
- ½ teaspoon ginger, minced
- 1 1/2 garlic cloves
- 1 green onion
- ½ teaspoon of rice wine vinegar
- ½ tablespoons Sriracha sauce
- ½ tablespoons sesame oil

Preparation:

1. At 390 degrees F, preheat your Air Fryer on Air fry mode.
2. Put all the ingredients for the marinade in the blender and blend them for 1 minute.
3. Keep this marinade aside. Pat dry the washed chicken and place it in the Ziploc bag.
4. Add buttermilk, chicken seasoning, and zip the bag.
5. Shake the bag well, then refrigerator for 30 minutes for marination.
6. Remove the chicken drumettes from the marinade, then dredge them through dry flour.
7. Spread the drumettes in the Air Fryer Basket and spray them with cooking oil.
8. Return the Air Fryer Basket to the Air Fryer and cook for 43 minutes.
9. Initiate cooking by pressing the START/PAUSE BUTTON.
10. Toss the drumettes once cooked halfway through.
11. Now brush the chicken pieces with Thai chili sauce and then resume cooking
12. Serve warm

Serving Suggestion: Serve with warm corn tortilla and ketchup.

Variation Tip: Rub the wings with lemon or orange juice before cooking.

Nutritional Information Per Serving:
Calories 223 | Fat 11.7g | Sodium 721mg | Carbs 13.6g | Fiber 0.7g | Sugar 8g | Protein 15.7g

Chicken Potatoes

Prep Time: 10 minutes.
Cook Time: 22 minutes.
Serves: 4

Ingredients:

- 15 ounces canned potatoes drained
- 1 teaspoon olive oil
- 1 teaspoon Lawry's seasoned salt
- 1/8 teaspoons black pepper optional
- 8 ounces boneless chicken breast cubed
- 1/4 teaspoons paprika
- 3/8 cup cheddar, shredded
- 4 bacon slices, cooked, cut into strips

Preparation:

1. At 300 degrees F, preheat your Air Fryer on Air fry mode.
2. Dice the chicken into small pieces and toss them with olive oil and spices.
3. Drain and dice the potato pieces into smaller cubes.
4. Add potato to the chicken and mix well to coat.
5. Spread the mixture in the Air Fryer Basket in a single layer.
6. Return the Air Fryer Basket to the Air Fryer and cook for 22 minutes.
7. Top the chicken and potatoes with cheese and bacon.
8. Return the Air Fryer Basket to the Air Fryer.
9. Select the Air Broil mode with 300 degrees F temperature and 5 minutes cooking time.
10. Initiate cooking by pressing the START/PAUSE BUTTON.
11. Enjoy with dried herbs on top.

Serving Suggestion: Serve with boiled white rice.

Variation Tip: Add sweet potatoes and green beans instead of potatoes.

Nutritional Information Per Serving:

Calories 346 | Fat 16.1g |Sodium 882mg | Carbs 1.3g | Fiber 0.5g | Sugar 0.5g | Protein 48.2g

Air Fried Turkey Breast

Prep Time: 10 minutes.
Cook Time: 46 minutes.
Serves: 4

Ingredients:

- 2 lbs. turkey breast, on the bone with skin
- ½ tablespoons olive oil
- 1 teaspoon salt
- 1/4 tablespoons dry poultry seasoning

Preparation:

1.   At 390 degrees F, preheat your Air Fryer on Air fry mode.
2.   Rub turkey breast with ½ tablespoons oil.
3.   Season both its sides with turkey seasoning and salt, then rub in the brush half tablespoons of oil over the skin of the turkey.
4.   Place the turkey in the Air Fryer Basket.
5.   Return the Air Fryer Basket to the Air Fryer and cook for 46 minutes.
6.   Initiate cooking by pressing the START/PAUSE BUTTON.
7.   Flip the turkey once cooked halfway through, and resume cooking.
8.   Slice and serve warm.

Serving Suggestion: Serve with warm corn tortilla and Greek salad.

Variation Tip: Coat and dust the turkey breast with flour after seasoning.

Nutritional Information Per Serving:
Calories 502 | Fat 25g |Sodium 230mg | Carbs 1.5g | Fiber 0.2g | Sugar 0.4g | Protein 64.1g

Chicken Drumettes

Prep Time: 15 minutes.
Cook Time: 52 minutes.
Serves: 5

Ingredients:

- 10 large chicken drumettes
- Cooking spray
- ¼ cup of rice vinegar
- 3 tablespoons honey
- 2 tablespoons unsalted chicken stock
- 1 tablespoon soy sauce
- 1 tablespoon toasted sesame oil
- 3/8 teaspoons crushed red pepper
- 1 garlic clove, chopped
- 2 tablespoons chopped unsalted roasted peanuts
- 1 tablespoon chopped fresh chives

Preparation:

1. At 390 degrees F, preheat your Air Fryer on Air fry mode.
2. Spread the chicken in the Air Fryer Basket in an even layer and spray cooking spray on top.
3. Return the Air Fryer Basket to the Air Fryer and cook for 47 minutes.
4. Initiate cooking by pressing the START/PAUSE BUTTON.
5. Flip the chicken drumettes once cooked halfway through, then resume cooking.
6. During this time, mix soy sauce, honey, stock, vinegar, garlic, and crushed red pepper in a suitable saucepan and place it over medium-high heat to cook on a simmer.
7. Cook this sauce for 6 minutes with occasional stirring, then pour it into a medium-sized bowl.
8. Add Air fried drumettes and toss well to coat with the honey sauce.
9. Garnish with chives and peanuts.
10. Serve warm and fresh

Serving Suggestion: Serve with tomato ketchup or chili sauce.

Variation Tip: Rub the chicken with lemon juice before seasoning.

Nutritional Information Per Serving:
Calories 268 | Fat 10.4g |Sodium 411mg | Carbs 0.4g | Fiber 0.1g | Sugar 0.1g | Protein 40.6g

Brazilian Chicken Drumsticks

Prep Time: 15 minutes.
Cook Time: 27 minutes.
Serves: 6

Ingredients:

- 2 teaspoons cumin seeds
- 2 teaspoons dried parsley
- 2 teaspoons turmeric powder
- 2 teaspoons dried oregano leaves
- 2 teaspoons salt
- 1 teaspoon coriander seeds
- 1 teaspoon black peppercorns
- 1 teaspoon cayenne pepper
- 1/2 cup lime juice
- 4 tablespoons vegetable oil
- 3 lbs chicken drumsticks

Preparation:

1. At 390 degrees F, preheat your Air Fryer on Air fry mode.
2. Grind cumin, parsley, salt, coriander seeds, cayenne pepper, peppercorns, oregano, and turmeric in a food processor.
3. Add this mixture to lemon juice and oil in a bowl and mix well.
4. Rub the spice paste over the chicken drumsticks and let them marinate for 30 minutes.
5. Place the chicken drumsticks in the Air Fryer Basket.
6. Return the Air Fryer Basket to the Air Fryer and cook for 27 minutes.
7. Initiate cooking by pressing the START/PAUSE BUTTON.
8. Flip the drumsticks when cooked halfway through, then resume cooking.
9. Serve warm.

Serving Suggestion: Serve with tomato ketchup or chili sauce.

Variation Tip: Use buttermilk to soak the drumsticks before seasoning.

Nutritional Information Per Serving:
Calories 456 | Fat 16.4g |Sodium 1321mg | Carbs 19.2g | Fiber 2.2g | Sugar 4.2g | Protein 55.2g

Bang-Bang Chicken

Prep Time: 15 minutes.
Cook Time: 20 minutes.
Serves: 2

Ingredients:

- 1 cup mayonnaise
- ½ cup sweet chili sauce
- 2 tablespoons Sriracha sauce
- ⅓ cup flour
- 1 lb boneless chicken breast, diced
- 1 ½ cups panko bread crumbs
- 2 green onions, chopped

Preparation:

1. At 390 degrees F, preheat your Air Fryer on Air fry mode.
2. Mix mayonnaise with Sriracha and sweet chili sauce in a large bowl.
3. Keep 3/4 cup of the mixture aside.
4. Add flour, chicken, breadcrumbs, and remaining mayo mixture to a resealable plastic bag.
5. Zip the bag and shake well to coat.
6. Place the chicken in the Air Fryer Basket in a single layer.
7. Return the Air Fryer Basket to the Air Fryer and cook for 20 minutes.
8. Initiate cooking by pressing the START/PAUSE BUTTON.
9. Flip the chicken once cooked halfway through.
10. Top the chicken with reserved mayo sauce.
11. Garnish with green onions and serve warm

Serving Suggestion: Serve with tomato ketchup or chili sauce.

Variation Tip: Use crushed cornflakes for breading to have extra crispiness.

Nutritional Information Per Serving:
Calories 374 | Fat 13g |Sodium 552mg | Carbs 25g | Fiber 1.2g | Sugar 1.2g | Protein 37.7g

Veggie Stuffed Chicken Breasts

Prep Time: 15 minutes.

Cook Time: 10 minutes.

Serves: 2

Ingredients:

- 4 teaspoons chili powder
- 4 teaspoons ground cumin
- 1 skinless, boneless chicken breast
- 2 teaspoons chipotle flakes
- 2 teaspoons Mexican oregano
- Salt and black pepper, to taste
- ½ red bell pepper, julienned
- ½ onion, julienned
- 1 fresh jalapeno pepper, julienned
- 2 teaspoons corn oil
- ½ lime, juiced

Preparation:

1. At 360 degrees F, preheat your Air Fryer on Air fry mode.
2. Slice the chicken breast in half horizontally.
3. Pound each chicken breast with a mallet into ¼ inch thickness.
4. Rub the pounded chicken breast with black pepper, salt, oregano, chipotle flakes, cumin, and chili powder.
5. Add ½ of bell pepper, jalapeno, and onion on top of each chicken breast piece.
6. Roll the chicken to wrap the filling inside and insert toothpicks to seal.
7. Place the rolls in the Air Fryer Basket and spray them with cooking oil.
8. Return the Air Fryer Basket to the Air Fryer and cook for 10 minutes.
9. Initiate cooking by pressing the START/PAUSE BUTTON.
10. Serve warm.

Serving Suggestion: Serve with tomato ketchup or chili sauce.

Variation Tip: season the chicken rolls with seasoned parmesan before cooking.

Nutritional Information Per Serving:

Calories 351 | Fat 11g | Sodium 150mg | Carbs 3.3g | Fiber 0.2g | Sugar 1g | Protein 33.2g

General Tso's Chicken

Prep Time: 20 minutes.
Cook Time: 22 minutes.
Serves: 4

Ingredients:

- 1 egg, large
- 1/3 cup 2 teaspoons cornstarch,
- 1/4 teaspoons salt
- 1/4 teaspoons ground white pepper
- 7 tablespoons chicken broth
- 2 tablespoons soy sauce
- 2 tablespoons ketchup
- 2 teaspoons sugar
- 2 teaspoons unseasoned rice vinegar
- 1 1/2 tablespoons canola oil
- 4 chilies de árbol, chopped and seeds discarded
- 1 tablespoon chopped fresh ginger
- 1 tablespoon garlic, chopped
- 2 tablespoons green onion, sliced
- 1 teaspoon toasted sesame oil
- 1 lb boneless chicken thighs, cut into 1 ¼ - inch chunks
- 1/2 teaspoons toasted sesame seeds

Preparation:

1. At 390 degrees F, preheat your Air Fryer on Air fry mode.
2. Add egg to a large bowl and beat it with a fork.
3. Add chicken to the egg and coat it well.
4. Whisk 1/3 cup cornstarch with black pepper and salt in a small bowl.
5. Add chicken to the cornstarch mixture and mix well to coat.
6. Place the chicken in the Air Fryer Basket and spray them with cooking oil.
7. Return the Air Fryer Basket to the Air Fryer and cook for 20 minutes.
8. Initiate cooking by pressing the START/PAUSE BUTTON.
9. Once done, remove the air fried chicken from the Air fryer.
10. Whisk 2 teaspoons cornstarch with soy sauce, broth, sugar, ketchup, and rice vinegar in a small bowl.
11. Add chilies and canola oil to a skillet and sauté for 1 minute.
12. Add garlic and ginger, then sauté for 30 seconds.
13. Stir in cornstarch sauce and cook until it bubbles and thickens.
14. Toss in cooked chicken and garnish with sesame oil, sesame seeds, and green onion.
15. Enjoy.

Serving Suggestion: Serve with boiled white rice or chow Mein.

Variation Tip: You can use honey instead of sugar to sweeten the sauce.

Nutritional Information Per Serving:
Calories 351 | Fat 16g |Sodium 777mg | Carbs 26g | Fiber 4g | Sugar 5g | Protein 28g

Bacon-Wrapped Chicken

Prep Time: 10 minutes.

Cook Time: 28 minutes.

Serves: 2

Ingredients:

- Butter:
- ½ stick butter softened
- ½ garlic clove, minced
- ¼ teaspoons dried thyme
- ¼ teaspoons dried basil
- ⅛ teaspoons coarse salt
- 1 pinch black pepper, ground
- ⅓ lb thick-cut bacon
- 1 ½ lbs boneless skinless chicken thighs
- 2 teaspoons garlic, minced

Preparation:

1. At 390 degrees F, preheat your Air Fryer on Air fry mode.
2. Mix garlic softened butter with thyme, salt, basil, and black pepper in a bowl.
3. Add butter mixture on a piece of wax paper and roll it up tightly to make a butter log.
4. Place the log in the refrigerator for 2 hours.
5. Spray one bacon strip on a piece of wax paper.
6. Place each chicken thigh on top of one bacon strip and rub it with garlic.
7. Make a slit in the chicken thigh and add a teaspoon of butter to the chicken.
8. Wrap the bacon around the chicken thigh.
9. Repeat those same steps with all the chicken thighs.
10. Place the bacon-wrapped chicken thighs in the Air Fryer Basket.
11. Return the Air Fryer Basket to the Air Fryer and cook for 28 minutes.
12. Initiate cooking by pressing the START/PAUSE BUTTON.
13. Flip the chicken once cooked halfway through, and resume cooking.
14. Serve warm

Serving Suggestion: Serve with tomato ketchup or chili sauce.

Variation Tip: Drizzle mixed dried herbs on top before cooking.

Nutritional Information Per Serving:

Calories 380 | Fat 29g | Sodium 821mg | Carbs 34.6g | Fiber 0g | Sugar 0g | Protein 30g

Cheddar- Stuffed Chicken

Prep Time: 10 minutes.
Cook Time: 20 minutes.
Serves: 4

Ingredients:

- 3 bacon strips, cooked and crumbled
- 2 ounces Cheddar cheese, cubed
- ¼ cup barbeque sauce
- 2 (4 ounces) boneless chicken breasts
- Salt and black pepper to taste

Preparation:

1. At 360 degrees F, preheat your Air Fryer on Air fry mode.
2. Make a 1-inch deep pouch in each chicken breast.
3. Mix cheddar cubes with half of the BBQ sauce, salt, black pepper, and bacon.
4. Divide this filling in the chicken breasts and secure the edges with a toothpick.
5. Brush the remaining BBQ sauce over the chicken breasts.
6. Place the chicken in the Air Fryer Basket and spray them with cooking oil.
7. Return the Air Fryer Basket to the Air Fryer and cook for 20 minutes.
8. Initiate cooking by pressing the START/PAUSE BUTTON.
9. Serve warm.

Serving Suggestion: Serve with tomato salsa on top.

Variation Tip: Use poultry seasoning for breading.

Nutritional Information Per Serving:
Calories 379 | Fat 19g |Sodium 184mg | Carbs 12.3g | Fiber 0.6g | Sugar 2g | Protein 37.7g

Balsamic Duck Breast

Prep Time: 15 minutes.

Cook Time: 20 minutes.

Serves: 2

Ingredients:

- 2 Duck Breasts
- 1 teaspoon parsley
- Salt and black pepper, to taste

Marinade:

- 1 tablespoon olive oil
- ½ teaspoon French mustard
- 1 teaspoon dried garlic
- 2 teaspoons honey
- ½ teaspoon Balsamic vinegar

Preparation:

1. At 360 degrees F, preheat your Air Fryer on Air fry mode.
2. Mix olive oil, mustard, garlic, honey, and balsamic vinegar in a bowl.
3. Add duck breasts to the marinade and rub well.
4. Place one duck breast in the Air Fryer Basket.
5. Return the Air Fryer Basket to the Air Fryer and cook for 20 minutes.
6. Initiate cooking by pressing the START/PAUSE BUTTON.
7. Flip the duck breasts once cooked halfway through, then resume cooking.
8. Serve warm.

Serving Suggestion: Serve with white rice and avocado salad

Variation Tip: Rub the duck breast with garlic cloves before seasoning.

Nutritional Information Per Serving:

Calories 546 | Fat 33.1g |Sodium 1201mg | Carbs 30g | Fiber 2.4g | Sugar 9.7g | Protein 32g

Beef, Pork, and Lamb Recipes

Air Fryer Meatloaves

Prep Time: 10 minutes.
Cook Time: 22 minutes.
Serves: 4

Ingredients:

- ⅓ cup milk
- 2 tablespoons basil pesto
- 1 egg, beaten
- 1 garlic clove, minced
- ¼ teaspoons black pepper
- 1 lb ground beef
- ⅓ cup panko bread crumbs
- 8 pepperoni slices
- ½ cup marinara sauce, warmed
- 1 tablespoon fresh basil, chopped

Preparation:

1. At 390 degrees F, preheat your Air Fryer on Air fry mode.
2. Mix pesto, milk, egg, garlic, and black pepper in a medium-sized bowl.
3. Stir in ground beef and bread crumbs, then mix.
4. Make the 4 small-sized loaves with this mixture and top them with 2 pepperoni slices.
5. Press the slices into the meatloaves.
6. Place the meatloaves in the Air Fryer Basket.
7. Return the Air Fryer Basket to the Air Fryer and cook for 22 minutes.
8. Initiate cooking by pressing the START/PAUSE BUTTON.
9. Top them with marinara sauce and basil to serve.
10. Serve warm.

Serving Suggestion: Serve with avocado dip.

Variation Tip: Add finely chopped carrots and zucchini to the meatloaf.

Nutritional Information Per Serving:
Calories 316 | Fat 12.2g |Sodium 587mg | Carbs 12.2g | Fiber 1g | Sugar 1.8g | Protein 25.8g

Chipotle Beef

Prep Time: 15 minutes.

Cook Time: 18 minutes.

Serves: 4

Ingredients:

- 1 lb beef steak, cut into chunks
- 1 large egg
- 1/2 cup parmesan cheese, grated
- 1/2 cup pork panko
- 1/2 teaspoons seasoned salt

Chipotle Ranch Dip

- 1/4 cup mayonnaise
- 1/4 cup sour cream
- 1 teaspoon chipotle paste
- 1/2 teaspoons ranch dressing mix
- 1/4 medium lime, juiced

Preparation:

1. At 390 degrees F, preheat your Air Fryer on Air fry mode.
2. Mix all the ingredients for chipotle ranch dip in a bowl.
3. Keep it in the refrigerator for 30 minutes.
4. Mix pork panko with salt and parmesan.
5. Beat egg in one bowl and spread the panko mixture in another flat bowl.
6. Dip the steak chunks in the egg first, then coat them with panko mixture.
7. Spread them in the Air Fryer Basket and spray them with cooking oil.
8. Return the Air Fryer Basket to the Air Fryer and cook for 18 minutes.
9. Initiate cooking by pressing the START/PAUSE BUTTON.
10. Serve with chipotle ranch and salt and pepper on top. Enjoy

Serving Suggestion: Serve with tomato ketchup or chili sauce.

Variation Tip: Add crushed cornflakes for breading to get extra crisp.

Nutritional Information Per Serving:

Calories 310 | Fat 17g |Sodium 271mg | Carbs 4.3g | Fiber 0.9g | Sugar 2.1g | Protein 35g

Zucchini Pork Skewers

Prep Time: 15 minutes.
Cook Time: 23 minutes.
Serves: 4

Ingredients:

- 1 large zucchini, cut 1" pieces
- 1 lb boneless pork belly, cut into cubes
- 1 onion yellow, diced in squares
- 1 ½ cup grape tomatoes
- 1 garlic clove minced
- 1 lemon, juice only
- 1/4 cup olive oil
- 2 tablespoons balsamic vinegar
- 1 teaspoon oregano
- olive oil spray

Preparation:

1. At 390 degrees F, preheat your Air Fryer on Air fry mode.
2. Mix together balsamic vinegar, garlic, oregano lemon juice, and 1/4 cup olive oil in a suitable bowl.
3. Then toss in diced pork pieces and mix well to coat.
4. Leave the seasoned pork to marinate for 60 minutes in the refrigerator.
5. Take suitable wooden skewers for your Air Fryer's Basket, and then thread marinated pork and vegetables on each skewer in an alternating manner.
6. Place the skewers in the Air Fryer Basket and spray them with cooking oil.
7. Return the Air Fryer Basket to the Air Fryer and cook for 23 minutes.
8. Initiate cooking by pressing the START/PAUSE BUTTON.
9. Flip the skewers once cooked halfway through, and resume cooking.
10. Serve warm.

Serving Suggestion: Serve with sautéed green beans and cherry tomatoes.

Variation Tip: Use honey glaze to baste the skewers.

Nutritional Information Per Serving:
Calories 459 | Fat 17.7g | Sodium 1516mg | Carbs 1.7g | Fiber 0.5g | Sugar 0.4g | Protein 69.2g

Pork with Green Beans and Potatoes

Prep Time: 10 minutes.

Cook Time: 25 minutes.

Serves: 4

Ingredients:

- ¼ cup Dijon mustard
- 2 tablespoons brown sugar
- 1 teaspoon dried parsley flake
- ½ teaspoon dried thyme
- ¼ teaspoons salt
- ¼ teaspoons black pepper
- 1 ¼ lb pork tenderloin
- ¾ lb small potatoes halved
- 1 (12 oz) package green beans, trimmed
- 1 tablespoon olive oil
- Salt and black pepper ground to taste

Preparation:

1. At 350 degrees F, preheat your Air Fryer on Air fry mode.
2. Add mustard, parsley, brown sugar, salt, black pepper, and thyme in a large bowl, then mix well.
3. Add tenderloin to the spice mixture and coat well.
4. Toss potatoes with olive oil, salt, black pepper, and green beans in another bowl.
5. Place the prepared tenderloin in the Air Fryer Basket.
6. Return the Air Fryer Basket to the Air Fryer and cook for 15 minutes.
7. Transfer the tenderloin to a plate and keep it covered.
8. Add potatoes and green beans to the Air Fryer Basket
9. Choose the Air Fryer mode with 350 degrees F temperature and 10 minutes cooking time.
10. Initiate cooking by pressing the START/PAUSE BUTTON.
11. Serve the tenderloin with Air Fried potatoes

Serving Suggestion: Serve with sautéed leeks or cabbages.

Variation Tip: Rub the tenderloins with garlic cloves before seasoning.

Nutritional Information Per Serving:

Calories 400 | Fat 32g |Sodium 721mg | Carbs 2.6g | Fiber 0g | Sugar 0g | Protein 27.4g

Beef Cheeseburgers

Prep Time: 15 minutes.
Cook Time: 13 minutes.
Serves: 4

Ingredients:

- 1 lb ground beef
- Salt, to taste
- 2 garlic cloves, minced
- 1 tablespoon soy sauce
- Black pepper, to taste
- 4 American cheese slices
- 4 hamburger buns
- Mayonnaise, to serve
- Lettuce, to serve
- Sliced tomatoes, to serve
- Sliced red onion, to serve

Preparation:

1. At 390 degrees F, preheat your Air Fryer on Air fry mode.
2. Mix beef with soy sauce and garlic in a large bowl.
3. Make 4 patties of 4 inches in diameter.
4. Rub them with salt and black pepper on both sides.
5. Place the patties in the Air Fryer Basket.
6. Return the Air Fryer Basket to the Air Fryer and cook for 13 minutes.
7. Initiate cooking by pressing the START/PAUSE BUTTON.
8. Flip each patty once cooked halfway through, and resume cooking.
9. Add each patty to the hamburger buns along with mayo, tomatoes, onions, and lettuce.
10. Serve

Serving Suggestion: Serve with tomato ketchup or chili sauce.

Variation Tip: Add breadcrumbs to the beef burger mixture for a crumbly texture.

Nutritional Information Per Serving:
Calories 437 | Fat 28g | Sodium 1221mg | Carbs 22.3g | Fiber 0.9g | Sugar 8g | Protein 30.3g

Mustard Rubbed Lamb Chops

Prep Time: 15 minutes.
Cook Time: 32 minutes.
Serves: 4

Ingredients:

- 1 teaspoon Dijon mustard
- 1 teaspoon olive oil
- ½ teaspoon soy sauce
- ½ teaspoon garlic, minced
- ½ teaspoon cumin powder
- ½ teaspoon cayenne pepper
- ½ teaspoon Italian spice blend
- 1/8 teaspoon salt
- 4 pieces of lamb chops

Preparation:

1. At 350 degrees F, preheat your Air Fryer on Air fry mode.
2. Mix Dijon mustard, soy sauce, olive oil, garlic, cumin powder, cayenne pepper, Italian spice blend, and salt in a medium bowl and mix well.
3. Place lamb chops into a Ziploc bag and pour in the marinade.
4. Press the air out of the bag and seal tightly.
5. Press the marinade around the lamb chops to coat.
6. Keep then in the fridge and marinate for at least 30 minutes, up to overnight.
7. Place the chops in the Air Fryer Basket and spray them with cooking oil.
8. Return the Air Fryer Basket to the Air Fryer and cook for 27 minutes.
9. Initiate cooking by pressing the START/PAUSE BUTTON.
10. Flip the chops once cooked halfway through, and resume cooking.
11. Switch the Air fryer to AIR broil mode and cook for 5 minutes.
12. Serve warm

Serving Suggestion: Serve the chops with a dollop of cream cheese dip on top.

Variation Tip: Rub the lamb chops with balsamic vinegar or honey before seasoning.

Nutritional Information Per Serving:
Calories 264 | Fat 17g |Sodium 129mg | Carbs 0.9g | Fiber 0.3g | Sugar 0g | Protein 27g

Lamb Shank with Mushroom Sauce

Prep Time: 15 minutes.
Cook Time: 35 minutes.
Serves: 4

Ingredients:

- 20 mushrooms, chopped
- 2 red bell pepper, chopped
- 2 red onion, chopped
- 1 cup red wine
- 4 leeks, chopped
- 6 tablespoons balsamic vinegar
- 2 teaspoons black pepper
- 2 teaspoons salt
- 3 tablespoons fresh rosemary
- 6 garlic cloves
- 4 lamb shanks
- 3 tablespoons olive oil

Preparation:

1. At 390 degrees F, preheat your Air Fryer on Air fry mode.
2. Season the lamb shanks with salt, pepper, rosemary, and 1 teaspoon olive oil.
3. Set the shanks in the Air Fryer Basket.
4. Return the Air Fryer Basket to the Air Fryer and cook for 25 minutes.
5. Initiate cooking by pressing the START/PAUSE BUTTON.
6. Flip the shanks halfway through, and resume cooking.
7. Meanwhile, add and heat the remaining olive oil in a skillet.
8. Add onion and garlic to sauté for 5 minutes.
9. Add in mushrooms and cook for 5 minutes.
10. Add red wine and cook until it is absorbed
11. Stir all the remaining vegetables along with black pepper and salt.
12. Cook until vegetables are al dente.
13. Serve the air fried shanks with sautéed vegetable fry.

Serving Suggestion: Serve with sautéed zucchini and green beans.

Variation Tip: Rub the lamb shanks with lemon juice before seasoning.

Nutritional Information Per Serving:
Calories 352 | Fat 9.1g |Sodium 1294mg | Carbs 3.9g | Fiber 1g | Sugar 1g | Protein 61g

Gochujang Brisket

Prep Time: 20 minutes.

Cook Time: 55 minutes.

Serves: 6

Ingredients:

- ½ tablespoons sweet paprika
- ½ teaspoon toasted sesame oil
- 2 lbs beef brisket, cut into 4 pieces
- Salt, to taste
- 1/8 cup Gochujang, Korean chili paste
- Black pepper, to taste
- 1 small onion, diced
- 2 garlic cloves, minced
- 1 teaspoon Asian fish sauce
- 1 ½ tablespoons peanut oil, as needed
- ½ tablespoons fresh ginger, grated
- ¼ teaspoons red chili flakes
- ½ cup of water
- 1 tablespoon ketchup
- 1 tablespoon soy sauce

Preparation:

1. At 390 degrees F, preheat your Air Fryer on Air fry mode.
2. Thoroughly rub the beef brisket with olive oil, paprika, chili flakes, black pepper, and salt.
3. Place the brisket in the Air Fryer Basket.
4. Return the Air Fryer Basket to the Air Fryer and cook for 35 minutes.
5. Initiate cooking by pressing the START/PAUSE BUTTON.
6. Flip the brisket halfway through, and resume cooking.
7. Meanwhile, heat oil in a skillet and add ginger, onion, and garlic.
8. Sauté for 5 minutes, then add all the remaining ingredients.
9. Cook the mixture for 15 minutes approximately until well thoroughly mixed.
10. Serve the brisket with this sauce on top.

Serving Suggestion: Serve on top of boiled white rice.

Variation Tip: Add Worcestershire sauce and honey to taste.

Nutritional Information Per Serving:

Calories 374 | Fat 25g |Sodium 275mg | Carbs 7.3g | Fiber 0g | Sugar 6g | Protein 12.3g

Pork Chops with Broccoli

Prep Time: 15 minutes.
Cook Time: 21 minutes.
Serves: 2

Ingredients:

- 2 (5 ounces) bone-in pork chops
- 2 tablespoons avocado oil
- 1/2 teaspoon paprika
- 1/2 teaspoon onion powder
- ½ teaspoon garlic powder
- 1 teaspoon salt
- 2 cups broccoli florets
- 2 garlic cloves, minced

Preparation:

1. At 375 degrees F, preheat your Air Fryer on Air fry mode.
2. Rub the pork chops with avocado oil, garlic, paprika, and spices.
3. Add pork chops to the Air Fryer Basket.
4. Return the Air Fryer Basket to the Air Fryer and cook for 15 minutes.
5. Transfer the chops to a plate and keep them covered.
6. Add the broccoli to the Air Fryer Basket and return it to the unit.
7. Choose the Air Fryer mode with 375 degrees F temperature and 6 minutes cooking time.
8. Initiate cooking by pressing the START/PAUSE BUTTON.
9. Flip the pork once cooked halfway through.
10. Cut the hardened butter into the cubes and place them on top of the pork chops.
11. Serve warm with crispy broccoli florets

Serving Suggestion: Serve with warm corn tortilla and crouton salad.

Variation Tip: Rub the pork chops with garlic cloves before seasoning.

Nutritional Information Per Serving:
Calories 410 | Fat 17.8g |Sodium 619mg | Carbs 21g | Fiber 1.4g | Sugar 1.8g | Protein 38.4g

Parmesan Pork Chops

Prep Time: 10 minutes.
Cook Time: 15 minutes.
Serves: 4

Ingredients:

- 4 boneless pork chops
- 2 tablespoons olive oil
- ½ cup freshly grated Parmesan
- 1 teaspoon salt
- 1 teaspoon paprika
- 1 teaspoon garlic powder
- 1 teaspoon onion powder
- ½ teaspoon black pepper

Preparation:

1. At 390 degrees F, preheat your Air Fryer on Air fry mode.
2. Pat dry the pork chops with a paper towel and rub them with olive oil.
3. Mix parmesan with spices in a medium bowl.
4. Rub the pork chops with Parmesan mixture.
5. Place the seasoned pork chops in the Air Fryer Basket.
6. Return the Air Fryer Basket to the Air Fryer and cook for 15 minutes.
7. Initiate cooking by pressing the START/PAUSE BUTTON.
8. Flip the pork chops when cooked halfway through, then resume cooking.
9. Serve warm.

Serving Suggestion: Serve boiled rice or steamed cauliflower rice.

Variation Tip: Rub the chops with garlic cloves before seasoning.

Nutritional Information Per Serving:
Calories 396 | Fat 23.2g |Sodium 622mg | Carbs 0.7g | Fiber 0g | Sugar 0g | Protein 45.6g

Turkey and Beef Meatballs

Prep Time: 15 minutes.
Cook Time: 24 minutes.
Serves: 6

Ingredients:

- 1 medium shallot, minced
- 2 tablespoons olive oil
- 3 garlic cloves, minced
- 1/4 cup panko crumbs
- 2 tablespoons whole milk
- 2/3 lb lean ground beef
- 1/3 lb bulk turkey sausage
- 1 large egg, lightly beaten
- ¼ cup parsley, chopped
- 1 tablespoon fresh thyme, chopped
- 1 tablespoon fresh rosemary, chopped
- 1 tablespoon Dijon mustard
- ½ teaspoon salt

Preparation:

1. At 400 degrees F, preheat your Air Fryer on Air fry mode.
2. Place a medium non-stick pan over medium-high heat.
3. Add oil and shallot, then sauté for 2 minutes.
4. Toss in the garlic and cook for 1 minute.
5. Remove this pan from the heat.
6. Whisk panko with milk in a large bowl and leave it for 5 minutes.
7. Add cooked shallot mixture and mix well.
8. Stir in egg, parsley, turkey sausage, beef, thyme, rosemary, salt, and mustard.
9. Mix well, then divide the mixture into 1 ½ inches balls.
10. Place these balls in the Air Fryer Basket and spray them with cooking oil.
11. Return the Air Fryer Basket to the Air Fryer and cook for 21 minutes.
12. Initiate cooking by pressing the START/PAUSE BUTTON.
13. Serve warm

Serving Suggestion: Serve with fresh vegetable salad and marinara sauce.

Variation Tip: Add freshly chopped parsley and coriander for change of taste.

Nutritional Information Per Serving:
Calories 551 | Fat 31g |Sodium 1329mg | Carbs 1.5g | Fiber 0.8g | Sugar 0.4g | Protein 64g

Pork Chops with Brussels Sprouts

Prep Time: 15 minutes.
Cook Time: 28 minutes.
Serves: 4

Ingredients:

- 4 bone-in center-cut pork chop
- Cooking spray
- Salt, to taste
- Black pepper, to taste
- 2 teaspoons olive oil
- 2 teaspoons pure maple syrup
- 2 teaspoons Dijon mustard
- 6 ounces Brussels sprouts, quartered

Preparation:

1. At 350 degrees F, preheat your Air Fryer on Air fry mode.
2. Rub pork chop with salt, ¼ teaspoons black pepper, and cooking spray.
3. Toss brussels sprouts with mustard, syrup, oil, ¼ teaspoons black pepper in a medium bowl.
4. Add pork chops to the Air Fryer Basket.
5. Return the Air Fryer Basket to the Air Fryer and cook for 15 minutes.
6. Transfer the pork chops to a plate and keep them covered.
7. Add the brussels sprouts to the basket and return it to the unit.
8. Choose the Air Fryer mode with 350 degrees F temperature and 13 minutes cooking time.
9. Initiate cooking by pressing the START/PAUSE BUTTON.
10. Serve warm and fresh

Serving Suggestion: Serve with Greek salad and crispy bread.

Variation Tip: Rub the pork chops with garlic cloves before seasoning.

Nutritional Information Per Serving:
Calories 336 | Fat 27.1g |Sodium 66mg | Carbs 1.1g | Fiber 0.4g | Sugar 0.2g | Protein 19.7g

Dessert Recipes

Apple Hand Pies

Prep Time: 15 minutes.

Cook Time: 21 minutes.

Serves: 8

Ingredients:

- 8 tablespoons butter, softened
- 12 tablespoons brown sugar
- 2 teaspoons cinnamon, ground
- 4 medium Granny Smith apples, diced
- 2 teaspoons cornstarch
- 4 teaspoons cold water
- 1 (14 oz) package pastry, 9-inch crust pie
- Cooking spray
- 1 tablespoon grapeseed oil
- ½ cup powdered sugar
- 2 teaspoons milk

Preparation:

1. At 390 degrees F, preheat your Air Fryer on Air fry mode.
2. Toss apples with brown sugar, butter, and cinnamon in a suitable skillet.
3. Place the skillet over medium heat and stir cook for 5 minutes.
4. Mix cornstarch with cold water in a small bowl.
5. Add cornstarch mixture into the apple and cook for 1 minute until it thickens.
6. Remove this filling from the heat and allow it to cool.
7. Unroll the pie crust and spray on a floured surface.
8. Cut the dough into 16 equal rectangles.
9. Wet the edges of the 8 rectangles with water and divide the apple filling at the center of these rectangles.
10. Place the other 8 rectangles on top and crimp the edges with a fork, then make 2-3 slashes on top.
11. Place the small pies in the Air Fryer Basket.
12. Return the Air Fryer Basket to the Air Fryer and cook for 17 minutes.
13. Initiate cooking by pressing the START/PAUSE BUTTON.
14. Flip the pies once cooked halfway through, and resume cooking.
15. Meanwhile, mix sugar with milk.
16. Pour this mixture over the apple pies.
17. Serve fresh.

Serving Suggestion: Serve with apple sauce.

Variation Tip: Add shredded nuts and coconuts to the filling.

Nutritional Information Per Serving:

Calories 284 | Fat 16g |Sodium 252mg | Carbs 31.6g | Fiber 0.9g | Sugar 6.6g | Protein 3.7g

Apple Nutmeg Flautas

Prep Time: 10 minutes.

Cook Time: 8 minutes.

Serves: 8

Ingredients:

- ¼ cup light brown sugar
- 1/8 cup all-purpose flour
- ¼ teaspoons ground cinnamon
- Nutmeg, to taste
- 4 apples, peeled, cored & sliced
- ½ lemon, juice, and zest
- 6 (10-inch) flour tortillas
- Vegetable oil
- Caramel sauce
- Cinnamon sugar

Preparation:

1. At 400 degrees F, preheat your Air Fryer on Air fry mode.
2. Mix brown sugar with cinnamon, nutmeg, and flour in a large bowl.
3. Toss in apples in lemon juice. Mix well.
4. Place a tortilla at a time on a flat surface and add ½ cup of the apple mixture to the tortilla.
5. Roll the tortilla into a burrito and seal it tightly and hold it in place with a toothpick.
6. Repeat the same steps with the remaining tortillas and apple mixture.
7. Place the apple burritos in the Air Fryer Basket and spray them with cooking oil.
8. Return the Air Fryer Basket to the Air Fryer and cook for 8 minutes.
9. Initiate cooking by pressing the START/PAUSE BUTTON.
10. Flip the burritos once cooked halfway through, then resume cooking.
11. Garnish with caramel sauce and cinnamon sugar.
12. Enjoy

Serving Suggestion: Serve with maple syrup on the side.

Variation Tip: Add orange juice and zest for change of taste.

Nutritional Information Per Serving:
Calories 157 | Fat 1.3g |Sodium 27mg | Carbs 1.3g | Fiber 1g | Sugar 2.2g | Protein 8.2g

Air Fried Beignets

Prep Time: 15 minutes.

Cook Time: 21 minutes.

Serves: 6

Ingredients:

- Cooking spray
- ¼ cup white sugar
- ⅛ cup water
- ½ cup all-purpose flour
- 1 large egg, separated
- 1 ½ teaspoon butter, melted
- ½ teaspoon baking powder
- ½ teaspoon vanilla extract
- 1 pinch salt
- 2 tablespoons confectioners' sugar, or to taste

Preparation:

1. At 390 degrees F, preheat your Air Fryer on Air fry mode.
2. Beat flour with water, sugar, egg yolk, baking powder, butter, vanilla extract, and salt in a large bowl until lumps-free.
3. Beat egg whites in a separate bowl and beat using an electric hand mixer until it forms soft peaks.
4. Add the egg white to the flour batter and mix gently until fully incorporated.
5. Divide the dough into small beignets and place them in the Air Fryer Basket.
6. Return the Air Fryer Basket to the Air Fryer and cook for 17 minutes.
7. Initiate cooking by pressing the START/PAUSE BUTTON.
8. And cook for another 4 minutes. Dust the cooked beignets with sugar.
9. Serve

Serving Suggestion: Serve with a dollop of sweet cream dip

Variation Tip: Add chopped raisins and nuts to the dough.

Nutritional Information Per Serving:

Calories 327 | Fat 14.2g |Sodium 672mg | Carbs 47.2g | Fiber 1.7g | Sugar 24.8g | Protein 4.4g

Air Fried Bananas

Prep Time: 10 minutes.
Cook Time: 13 minutes.
Serves: 4

Ingredients:

- 4 bananas, sliced
- 1 avocado oil cooking spray

Preparation:

1. At 350 degrees F, preheat your Air Fryer on Air fry mode.
2. Spread the banana slices in the Air Fryer Basket in a single layer.
3. Drizzle avocado oil over the banana slices.
4. Return the Air Fryer Basket to the Air Fryer and cook for 13 minutes.
5. Initiate cooking by pressing the START/PAUSE BUTTON.
6. Serve

Serving Suggestion: Serve with a dollop of vanilla ice-cream.

Variation Tip: Drizzle chopped nuts on top of the bananas

Nutritional Information Per Serving:
Calories 149 | Fat 1.2g |Sodium 3mg | Carbs 37.6g | Fiber 5.8g | Sugar 29g | Protein 1.1g

Apple Crisp

Prep Time: 15 minutes.
Cook Time: 14 minutes.
Serves: 8

Ingredients:

- 3 cups apples, chopped
- 1 tablespoon pure maple syrup
- 2 teaspoons lemon juice
- 3 tablespoons all-purpose flour
- 1/3 cup quick oats
- ¼ cup brown sugar
- 2 tablespoons light butter, melted
- ½ teaspoon cinnamon

Preparation:

1. At 375 degrees F, preheat your Air Fryer on Air fry mode.
2. Toss the chopped apples with 1 tablespoon of all-purpose flour, cinnamon, maple syrup, and lemon juice in a suitable bowl.
3. Add the apples in the Air Fryer Basket with its crisper plate.
4. Whisk oats, brown sugar, and remaining all-purpose flour in a small bowl.
5. Stir in melted butter, then spread this mixture over the apples.
6. Return the Air Fryer Basket to the Air Fryer and cook for 14 minutes.
7. Initiate cooking by pressing the START/PAUSE BUTTON.
8. Enjoy fresh

Serving Suggestion: Serve with a warming cup of hot chocolate.

Variation Tip: Use crushed cookies or graham crackers instead of oats.

Nutritional Information Per Serving:
Calories 258 | Fat 12.4g |Sodium 79mg | Carbs 34.3g | Fiber 1g | Sugar 17g | Protein 3.2g

Zesty Cranberry Scones

Prep Time: 10 minutes.
Cook Time: 16 minutes.
Serves: 8

Ingredients:

- 4 cups of flour
- 1/2 cup brown sugar
- 2 tablespoons baking powder
- ½ teaspoon ground nutmeg
- ½ teaspoon salt
- ½ cup butter, chilled and diced
- 2 cups fresh cranberry
- 2/3 cup sugar
- 2 tablespoons orange zest
- 1 ¼ cup half and half cream
- 2 eggs

Preparation:

1. At 375 degrees F, preheat your Air Fryer on Air fry mode.
2. Whisk flour with baking powder, salt, nutmeg, and both the sugars in a bowl.
3. Stir in egg and cream, mix well to form a smooth dough.
4. Fold in cranberries along with the orange zest.
5. Knead this dough well on a work surface.
6. Cut 3-inch circles out of the dough.
7. Place the scones in the Air Fryer Basket and spray them with cooking oil.
8. Return the Air Fryer Basket to the Air Fryer and cook for 16 minutes.
9. Initiate cooking by pressing the START/PAUSE BUTTON.
10. Flip the scones once cooked halfway and resume cooking.
11. Enjoy

Serving Suggestion: Serve with cranberry jam on the side.

Variation Tip: Add raisins instead of cranberries to the dough.

Nutritional Information Per Serving:
Calories 204 | Fat 9g |Sodium 91mg | Carbs 27g | Fiber 2.4g | Sugar 15g | Protein 1.3g

Walnuts Fritters

Prep Time: 15 minutes.

Cook Time: 15 minutes.

Serves: 6

Ingredients:

- 1 cup all-purpose flour
- ½ cup walnuts, chopped
- ¼ cup white sugar
- ¼ cup milk
- 1 egg
- 1 ½ teaspoon baking powder
- 1 pinch salt
- Cooking spray
- 2 tablespoons white sugar
- ½ teaspoon ground cinnamon

Glaze:

- ½ cup confectioners' sugar
- 1 tablespoon milk
- ½ teaspoon caramel extract
- ¼ teaspoons ground cinnamon

Preparation:

1. At 375 degrees F, preheat your Air Fryer on Air fry mode.
2. Layer the Air Fryer Basket with parchment paper.
3. Grease the parchment paper with cooking spray.
4. Whisk flour with milk, 1/4 cup sugar, egg, baking powder, and salt in a small bowl.
5. Separately mix 2 tablespoons sugar with cinnamon in another bowl, toss in walnuts and mix well to coat.
6. Stir in flour mixture and mix until combined.
7. Drop the fritters mixture using a cookie scoop into the Air Fryer Basket.
8. Return the Air Fryer Basket to the Air Fryer and cook for 15 minutes.
9. Initiate cooking by pressing the START/PAUSE BUTTON.
10. Flip the fritters once cooked halfway through, then resume cooking.
11. Meanwhile, whisk milk, caramel extract, confectioners' sugar, and cinnamon in a bowl.
12. Transfer fritters to a wire rack and allow them to cool.
13. Drizzle with a glaze over the fritters

Serving Suggestion: Serve with butter pecan ice cream or strawberry jam.

Variation Tip: Add maple syrup on top.

Nutritional Information Per Serving:
Calories 391 | Fat 24g |Sodium 142mg | Carbs 38.5g | Fiber 3.5g | Sugar 21g | Protein 6.6g

Oreo Rolls

Prep Time: 10 minutes.
Cook Time: 12 minutes.
Serves: 9

Ingredients:

- 1 crescent sheet roll
- 9 Oreo cookies
- Cinnamon powder, to serve
- Powdered sugar, to serve

Preparation:

1. At 360 degrees F, preheat your Air Fryer on Air fry mode.
2. Spread the crescent sheet roll and cut it into 9 equal squares.
3. Place one cookie at the center of each square.
4. Wrap each square around the cookies and press the ends to seal.
5. Place half of the wrapped cookies in the Air Fryer Basket.
6. Return the Air Fryer Basket to the Air Fryer and cook for 6 minutes.
7. Initiate cooking by pressing the START/PAUSE BUTTON.
8. Cook the remaining cookie rolls in the same way.
9. Garnish the rolls with sugar and cinnamon.
10. Serve.

Serving Suggestion: Serve a cup of spice latte or hot chocolate.

Variation Tip: Dip the rolls in melted chocolate for a change of taste.

Nutritional Information Per Serving:
Calories 175 | Fat 13.1g | Sodium 154mg | Carbs 14g | Fiber 0.8g | Sugar 8.9g | Protein 0.7g

Biscuit Doughnuts

Prep Time: 15 minutes.
Cook Time: 15 minutes.
Serves: 8

Ingredients:

- ½ cup white sugar
- 1 teaspoon cinnamon
- ½ cup powdered sugar
- 1 can pre-made biscuit dough
- Coconut oil
- Melted butter to brush biscuits

Preparation:

1. At 375 degrees F, preheat your Air Fryer on Air fry mode.
2. Place all the biscuits on a cutting board and cut holes in the center of each biscuit using a cookie cutter.
3. Grease the Air Fryer Basket with coconut oil.
4. Place the biscuits in the Air Fryer Basket while keeping them 1 inch apart.
5. Return the Air Fryer Basket to the Air Fryer and cook for 15 minutes.
6. Initiate cooking by pressing the START/PAUSE BUTTON.
7. Brush all the donuts with melted butter and sprinkle cinnamon and sugar on top.
8. Air fry these donuts for one minute more.
9. Enjoy

Serving Suggestion: Serve the doughnuts with chocolate syrup on top.

Variation Tip: Inject strawberry jam into each doughnut.

Nutritional Information Per Serving:
Calories 192 | Fat 9.3g |Sodium 133mg | Carbs 27.1g | Fiber 1.4g | Sugar 19g | Protein 3.2g

21 Days Meal Plan

Week 1

Monday:

Breakfast: Morning Patties

Lunch: Sweet Potatoes with Honey Butter

Snack: Fried Olives

Dinner: Mustard Rubbed Lamb Chops

Dessert: Walnuts Fritters

Tuesday

Breakfast: Crispy Hash Browns

Lunch: Air Fried Okra

Snack: Crispy Plantain Chips

Dinner: Zucchini Pork Skewers

Dessert: Apple Hand Pies

Wednesday

Breakfast: Air Fried Sausage

Lunch: Quinoa Patties

Snack: Peppered Asparagus

Dinner: Chipotle Beef

Dessert: Air Fried Bananas

Thursday

Breakfast: Pepper Egg Cups

Lunch: Zucchini Cakes

Snack: Cauliflower Gnocchi

Dinner: Gochujang Brisket

Dessert: Air Fried Beignets

Friday

Breakfast: Breakfast Bacon

Lunch: Saucy Carrots

Snack: Fried Halloumi Cheese

Dinner: Lamb Shank with Mushroom Sauce

Dessert: Biscuit Doughnuts

Saturday

Breakfast: Biscuit Balls

Lunch: Falafel

Snack: Crispy Tortilla Chips

Dinner: Beef Cheeseburgers

Dessert: Zesty Cranberry Scones

Sunday

Breakfast: Morning Egg Rolls

Lunch: Lime Glazed Tofu

Snack: Parmesan French Fries

Dinner: Parmesan Pork Chops

Dessert: Apple Nutmeg Flautas

Week 2

Monday:

Breakfast: Spinach Egg Muffins

Lunch: Chicken Drumettes

Snack: Chicken Crescent Wraps

Dinner: Pork Chops with Broccoli

Dessert: Apple Crisp

Tuesday

Breakfast: Pumpkin Muffins

Lunch: General Tso's Chicken

Snack: Chicken Stuffed Mushrooms

Dinner: Turkey and Beef Meatballs

Dessert: Oreo Rolls

Wednesday

Breakfast: Cinnamon Toasts

Lunch: Bang-Bang Chicken

Snack: Onion Rings

Dinner: Pork Chops with Brussels Sprouts

Dessert: Apple Nutmeg Flautas

Thursday

Breakfast: Morning Patties

Lunch: Bacon-Wrapped Chicken

Snack: Potato Tater Tots

Dinner: Air Fryer Meatloaves

Dessert: Apple Crisp

Friday

Breakfast: Crispy Hash Browns

Lunch: Crumbed Chicken Katsu

Snack: Crispy Plantain Chips

Dinner: Pork with Green Beans and Potatoes

Dessert: Oreo Rolls

Saturday

Breakfast: Air Fried Sausage

Lunch: Breaded Scallops

Snack: Peppered Asparagus

Dinner: Veggie Stuffed Chicken Breasts

Dessert: Apple Hand Pies

Sunday

Breakfast: Pepper Egg Cups

Lunch: Salmon Nuggets

Snack: Cauliflower Gnocchi

Dinner: Cheddar- Stuffed Chicken

Dessert: Walnuts Fritters

Week 3

Monday:

Breakfast: Breakfast Bacon

Lunch: Crispy Catfish

Snack: Fried Halloumi Cheese

Dinner: Balsamic Duck Breast

Dessert: Air Fried Bananas

Tuesday

Breakfast: Biscuit Balls

Lunch: Crusted Tilapia

Snack: Crispy Tortilla Chips

Dinner: Brazilian Chicken Drumsticks

Dessert: Air Fried Beignets

Wednesday

Breakfast: Morning Egg Rolls

Lunch: Glazed Scallops

Snack: Parmesan French Fries

Dinner: Chili Chicken Wings

Dessert: Biscuit Doughnuts

Thursday

Breakfast: Spinach Egg Muffins

Lunch: Crusted Cod

Snack: Chicken Crescent Wraps

Dinner: Air Fried Turkey Breast

Dessert: Zesty Cranberry Scones

Friday

Breakfast: Pumpkin Muffins

Lunch: Savory Salmon Fillets

Snack: Chicken Stuffed Mushrooms

Dinner: Chicken Potatoes

Dessert: Apple Nutmeg Flautas

Saturday

Breakfast: Morning Patties

Lunch: Salmon with Fennel Salad

Snack: Onion Rings

Dinner: Pickled Chicken Fillets

Dessert: Apple Crisp

Sunday

Breakfast: Crispy Hash Browns

Lunch: Buttered Mahi Mahi

Snack: Potato Tater Tots

Dinner: Crusted Chicken Breast

Dessert: Oreo Rolls

Conclusion

A smart Air Fryer has become the need of today. Gone are the days when people could rely on deep oil frying; as we are living in the age of tech-smart kitchen appliances now, Air frying can offer the same results without the use of excess oil. The Air frying cooking technique is much healthier and cooks crispy food every time with low-fat content. Ninja food tech company has therefore launched its own series of Air Fryers, which can offer even frying at any temperature. The shape of the appliance gives it an extra edge over the other competing models in the market, as it has a broad base containing sufficient space inside its cooking basket. To make the device more versatile in its function, it comes with manually controlled temperature and timing operations, whereas there are also other modes of cooking available that provide preset settings. This Ninja Air fryer cookbook is designed to highlight several of its other amazing features while providing a range of recipes that can be cooked using this Air fryer. If you are always in the mood to enjoy some crisp, then Ninja Air fryer is all for you, and this cookbook can be your ultimate guide.

By looking at the control panel of the ninja Air fryer, you will realize how simple and user-friendly its mechanism is. You don't need to constantly check and set the hardware or the software. Just plug it in and select the desired mode, time, and temperature, and press start. By its single-button technology, it gives easier access to all of its users. The preset modes allow even easier handling of the device. The assembly of all of its accessories, from the Air Fryer Basket to the crisper plate and the rack, is also quite simple. Follow the steps discussed above, and anyone can become the Ninja Air fryer expert. It takes just 2 to 3 sessions of cooking with the device to fully understand its control.

The Ninja Air fryer is not completely an Air fryer like other companies offer in the market. Besides the Air frying mode, it also offers other modes of cooking, including the roasting mode, the reheating, and dehydrating mode. The cooking techniques used in this device are also appropriate for roasting food and dehydrating it. So, let's get started with some smart oil-free cooking!